Contents

INTRODUCTION

The data problem

Every business, even a start-up or small or medium-sized enterprise (SME), has data.

Think about these:

- the data you collect on your customers;
- your website, email and social media data;
- your financial data, showing money in and money out;
- the data you collect on your employees;
- the platforms and third-party tools you use;
- and so on.

Once a business has even a handful of employees, you'll have islands of data, including from the following:

- financial system;
- web analytics tool;
- email marketing tool;
- social media platforms;
- customer relationship management (CRM) tool;
- e-commerce platform;
- human resources (HR) system;
- payroll tool;

- databases;
- cloud data storage solution;
- a ton of Microsoft Excel spreadsheets;
- and more.

The larger the business, the more data islands you'll have.

And this is where the problem starts – most businesses have disparate, disconnected data. They don't have a single version of the truth. Everyone within the business quotes different numbers, which causes a mistrust of any data facts, information and statistics shared. So, data feels like a problem.

The data risk

On top of the data problem, working with data can be high risk, particularly when you're working with confidential, commercially sensitive data or personally identifiable information (PII).

We've all seen news reports on data hacks, thefts and loss – these events result in press coverage, reputational damage, loss of customers, and fines. So, data security needs to be at the front of everyone's minds, when it comes to a data project (see *Storing Data* section later in the book).

The data opportunity

Businesses can make or save money using data.

Think about these:

- seeing all your data in one place, so you can spot opportunities and problems quickly and easily;
- identifying where to cut costs using data;
- seeing where business results are good or bad across your business, so you can target your effort in the right places;
- combining data across your business to identify cross-departmental opportunities;

- using data to personalise your products and services for your clients;
- creating brand-new products and services for your current customers or for new markets;
- providing all your staff with a single view of a customer, employee, product or another business asset; and
- monetising your data and creating brand-new revenue streams.

Most businesses can increase their profit by at least 10% using data they already have in their business, and what business doesn't want to increase its profit?

Yet data skills, experience and knowledge are hard to find; they're in high demand, but low supply, so they're an expensive and rare commodity.

So where do you start?

The data solution

Your business can ride the Data Escalator TODAY using this step-by-step guide. I have broken down all the different things you'll need to consider when it comes to data into eight simple steps:

- ✶ **STEP #1** – Understand your business needs
- ✶ **STEP #2** – Define your data strategy
- ✶ **STEP #3** – Map your data sources
- ✶ **STEP #4** – Connect your data
- ✶ **STEP #5** – Process your data
- ✶ **STEP #6** – Analyse your data
- ✶ **STEP #7** – Visualise your data
- ✶ **STEP #8** – Monetise your data

This Data Escalator will enable you to do the following:

✓ Apply big-business strategies to your SME business
✓ Take advantage of cutting-edge technology and tools
✓ Monetise data to power your business growth

The Data Escalator will help you to *make more money using data you already have in your business.*

Who's this book for?

Are you a business owner?

A business leader?

An innovator?

An entrepreneur?

You can make more money for your business in eight simple steps.

You can use data you already have *within* your business:

✓ to transform your business;
✓ to make smarter, quicker decisions; and
✓ to earn more money.

The eight-step Data Escalator was inspired by a team of data consultants, architects, engineers, analysts, visualisers and scientists, who work with UK and global organisations every day.

And I make a promise to you: **there is no jargon and no theories, just super-practical tools to enable you to grow your business using data.**

Here are the eight steps on the Data Escalator:

* **STEP #1 – UNDERSTAND YOUR BUSINESS NEEDS**

  If you don't know the 'why', forget about the 'how', 'when' and 'what'

  Step #1 is all about ensuring your data work is purposeful and results in valuable, actionable insight. This begins with understanding what your objectives are, what you're trying to achieve and what 'good' looks like BEFORE starting any data work.

* **STEP #2 – DEFINE YOUR DATA STRATEGY**

  If you don't know where you're going, you'll never get there

  Step #2 is to create a data strategy that's aligned to your business strategy and sets out a clear vision for your business to achieve. This starts with reviewing your business strategy and the data insight that exists regarding your business right now.

* **STEP #3 – MAP YOUR DATA SOURCES**

  If you don't know what data is available, you'll miss the good stuff

  Step #3 involves identifying, reviewing and mapping your data sources to your business needs, so you'll understand what data you can play with. This covers internal vs external data and structured vs unstructured data.

* **STEP #4 – CONNECT YOUR DATA**

  If you don't know where the dots are, you'll never join them up

  Step #4 is focused on extracting your data and connecting it all together. This includes finding unique identifiers to match your data perfectly.

* STEP #5 – PROCESS YOUR DATA

If you don't know the risks, you can't mitigate them

Step #5 is to transform, prepare and sort your data, so it's ready for analysis. This starts with ensuring your data is secure, compliant and robust.

* STEP #6 – ANALYSE YOUR DATA

If you don't try, you'll never know

Step #6 involves analysing your data to find new patterns and trends. This covers descriptive, comparative and predictive analytics, as well as using artificial intelligence (AI) and statistical tools.

* STEP #7 – VISUALISE YOUR DATA

If it doesn't tell you something, what's the point?

Step #7 is to visualise your data to enable you to present intuitive designs and insight to your target users. This includes considering the types of visualisations, graphs, imagery and tools you can use.

* STEP #8 – MONETISE YOUR DATA

If there's no business benefit, why bother?

Step #8 is using your data to make or save more money, in a compliant and customer-focused way. This starts with thinking about who would value your data and what they'd do with it.

How to read this book

This book is designed as a step-by-step guide, following a logical eight-step process. This process can work for any business and for any data project; it starts with a data requirement and continues all the way through to the delivery of a data solution. But, if you prefer, you can jump forward to any of the steps on the Data Escalator that you want to focus on. Take care not to miss Step #1, though; understanding your business needs is one step you musn't miss, as it defines what you need to deliver in order to create business value. Other than that, you can dive in and out of the book and each step on the Data Escalator whenever/wherever you like. Use this book in whatever way works for you and your business.

INTRODUCING REAL-WORLD EXAMPLES

Each step on the Data Escalator includes some real-world examples for our readers; this is where I share case studies showing how each of the steps have been climbed in the business world. This turns the theory into practical, tactical examples to bring it to life for you.

INTRODUCING LESSONS LEARNT

Each step on the Data Escalator ends with some lessons learnt; this is where I share the benefit of my experience of working on tons of data projects, getting things wrong and learning better ways to do things. I want you to learn from my experience, so you don't make the same mistakes I did.

INTRODUCING TASKS

Each step on the Data Escalator also ends with a task; these practical, tactical actions will enable you to create a data plan that you can implement within your business. They're designed to get you started and give you a structure to work with. I recommend you do these tasks straight away after reading each step, so they're fresh in your mind. You can always start them now and finish them later.

After riding the eight steps of the Data Escalator, you'll be able to do the following:

✓ Create a data strategy and plan for your business
✓ Launch your first data project
✓ Know what good data looks like

So what are you waiting for? *Let's begin.*

STEP #1

UNDERSTAND YOUR BUSINESS NEEDS

If you don't know the 'why', forget about the 'how', 'when' and 'what'

STEP #1 – UNDERSTAND YOUR BUSINESS NEEDS

Data is meaningless without a purpose. It's just numbers, words and statistics. To derive meaningful insight from data, you need to start with your business needs. You need to understand WHY people will benefit from using data: what they need to be able to see in the data, what they need to be able to do with the data, what they'll do differently when they see the data, what actions they'll take once they understand the insight derived from the data, what they'll stop/start doing and what changes they'll make using the data. You need to spend a significant amount of time understanding the business needs for data before you can start work.

STOP! Walk away from the data

Don't start with the data. Whilst it's tempting to extract data, start playing with it and create some graphs – don't! You'll drown in the data, you'll answer questions you already know, you'll do things in the same way you've always done them, and you'll create meaningless, unhelpful and unused data reports. Instead, start with the business needs: a goal, an end game, a hypothesis or a challenge.

Right at the very start is where I often see data projects go wrong. They jump straight into the data and don't take the time up front to consider why they're doing a project, how it could benefit the business and what decisions could be made using the insight derived from the data. And the inevitable happens: if you don't understand the business needs, your output at the end risks being solely a load of pretty pictures or a stream of mildly interesting facts and figures. A data output that no one uses and everyone forgets is a waste of your time. Don't make this common mistake. Invest time in the start of your project to really understand what your business needs BEFORE touching the data.

Data vs insight

Let's start with the definitions:

* **Data** – 'Facts and statistics collected together for reference or analysis.'[1]

* **Insight** – 'The capacity to gain an accurate and deep understanding of someone or something.'[2]

Data on its own isn't valuable to a business. It's just facts or statistics. What's beneficial is the power of data to enable the creation of new insight for a business: to further your understanding, to tell you something new, to challenge previously held assumptions, or to discover new patterns and trends. That's when data becomes meaningful, valuable and an important business asset.

To derive actionable insight from data, let's start with the reasons why you'll want to explore data in the first place – your business needs.

A business need could be one of the following:

a. **To answer a specific question or a set of questions**

For instance:

* Who are our highest-value customers?

* Who are our lowest-value customers?

* Have any high-value customers changed to be low-value customers in the last year?

* Have any low-value customers changed to be high-value customers in the last year?

---

1. Data (n.d.). In Lexico.com dictionary. Retrieved from https://www.lexico.com/definition/data

2. Insight (n.d.). In Lexico.com dictionary. Retrieved from https://www.lexico.com/definition/insight

b. To inform a decision

For instance:

- Should we invest in X or Y?
- Should we recruit more people in location #1 or location #2?
- Should we cut costs in department A or B?
- Should we increase marketing spend on product #1 or #2?

c. To test a hypothesis or a set of hypotheses

For instance:

- Product #1 is more profitable than product #2
- Sales conversion rates are higher in region A than region B
- LinkedIn generates more leads than Facebook
- The cost per acquisition is higher for product #1 than product #2

d. To track actuals vs targets

For instance:

- Are we on track to achieve our sales target at the end of the year?
- Will our costs be within budget at this run rate?
- How different are sales-conversion-rate targets to actuals?
- Which region is the furthest from its sales-volume target?

e. To discover new patterns and trends

For instance:

- Tell us something we don't know about our business
- What's influencing our sales performance at a regional level?
- How have our product sales varied over the last five years?
- Why has customer satisfaction fallen in the last year?

A good way to derive these business needs from your business stakeholders is to ask them questions such as the following:

* What do you wish you knew about your business that you don't know today?

* Is there a hypothesis, assumption or urban myth about your business that you've never verified with data?

* If we could tell you one thing about your business/department using data, what would it be?

In my experience, although they might struggle at first, once people start coming up with data questions, they never stop!

Business needs by function

Your data project needs to focus more on generating insight than sharing data. However, insight is in the eye of the beholder. Insight means different things to different people. Your chief executive officer (CEO) will have a different view of what insight looks like than your sales director, your customer services manager or your head of HR, so you need to identify your primary data user before you begin.

Depending on their roles in the business, your business stakeholders will be interested in different types of business metrics and potential areas of insight:

FINANCIAL	SALES	PRODUCT	CUSTOMER	MARKETING	EFFICIENCY	PEOPLE
Revenue	Volumes	Categories/ types	Acquisition	Response rates	Resources	Volumes
Cost	Leads	Pricing	Purchasing frequency	Visitors	Process	Types
Profit	Conversion	Profit	Customer lifetime value	Market share	Time vs effort	Costs
Investment			Service level agreements (SLAs)	Share of voice		New recruits
Cashflow			Engagement	Brand awareness		Performance
			Satisfaction	Loyalty		Satisfaction
			Retention			Attrition

This means you'll need to tailor your data project depending on which business stakeholder you're talking to and focus on the areas that matter to them. Of course, at the board or senior leadership level, your stakeholders could be interested in all these business areas, but at a summarised level of detail. Whilst it's tempting to try to make everyone happy and include all business needs within one data project, rarely does one size fit all. I highly recommend you focus on one business user, or department, at a time; deliver an awesome data project for them; and then move on to other business areas.

The three business levers

At a simplistic level, there are only three actions you can take within a business to improve your business performance:

1. **You can STOP an activity**

2. **You can START an activity**

3. **You can CHANGE an activity**

Here are some examples of the types of actions you can take:

1. **You can STOP an activity**

- Exit a market
- Remove a product
- Close an office
- Stop expenditure
- Stop a campaign
- Stop recruitment

2. **You can START an activity**

- Launch into a new market
- Launch a product
- Open an office
- Invest in a new area
- Launch a campaign
- Recruit people

3. **You can CHANGE an activity**

- You can spend more/less
  - Change budget allocation
  - Change marketing tactics

- You can add/remove resources
  - Change resource allocation
  - Recruit in some areas and cut staff in others

- You can change a process/methodology
  - Improve efficiency
  - Add controls and governance
  - Add/remove intermediaries
  - Add/remove tools and platforms

Before you start your data project, it's crucial that you understand what business levers your users can pull or push as a result of acquiring the new insight derived from the data in your project. This will ensure that your data project will deliver not just insight but actionable insight – that is, something that can be acted upon and implemented within your business. Insight that can be used to help your business to perform better.

Let's take some of the previous examples of business needs and explore the associated business levers:

BUSINESS NEED	BUSINESS LEVERS
Who are our highest-value customers?	Marketing can use this insight to do the following: • target communications to a specific customer segment; • change communication channels; or • change budget allocation.
Should we invest in X or Y?	Finance can use this insight to do the following: • stop spending in some areas; • start spending in other areas; and • justify decisions to the board.

BUSINESS NEED	BUSINESS LEVERS
Is product #1 more profitable than product #2?	Product can use this insight to do the following: • remove a product; • change the pricing for a product; or • change the product offering.
Are we on track to achieve our sales target at the end of the year?	Sales can use this insight to do the following: • change the number of salespeople; • change the sales incentive scheme; or • change the spend on sales collateral or lead-generation activity.
Where has customer satisfaction fallen in the last year?	The board can use this insight to do the following: • change the customer service model; • change the distributor model; or • target the problem areas for investment.

In my experience, stakeholders can struggle with this exercise as it can feel theoretical and abstract at the start; what will you do with unknown, unexpected data insight? It can be hard to answer, so here are some tips:

- Ask them what they'll do when they get the insight from the data project:
    - *Who will they tell?*
    - *Why?*
    - *When?*

- Share some hypothetical examples with them, to make it real; for instance, the following:

    o If the data shows that customer satisfaction has declined in the last year, what will you do?

    o If the data shows that the highest-value customers are at risk of leaving you, what will you do?

    o If the data shows the campaign has generated fewer than 10 leads, what will you do?

It's also useful to ask them what resource, budget and/or process actions they might take, and be prepared to give them some examples if they need a prompt.

This is a crucial step to ensuring you understand WHY they need data insight and not just WHAT data insight they need. So be prepared to probe, ask lots of questions, be curious and fully explore the real reasons why they need data insight.

Prioritising business needs

When you start this process, you're likely to have one or two business needs to explore. However, as time goes on, the business needs will grow within your organisation and, eventually, you'll have far too many business needs to explore with limited resources and budget. That's when you'll need a way to prioritise your business needs and decide which ones to explore first.

When deciding on priorities, there are three questions you can ask your stakeholders:

* *Will the data insight help the business to make or save money?*

* *Will the data insight help the business to win or retain more clients?*

* *Will the data insight give the business a strategic advantage?*

This approach focuses on the commercial business value of insight generation. It will help you to filter out the projects that are simply interesting from the projects that could help your business grow faster.

Here's a repeatable method you can use to assess the commercial business value of each business need:

#	QUESTION		SCORE	RESULT
1.	Will the data insight help your business to make or save money?	No directly attributable cost savings or revenue potential	0	
		< £10k per annum (pa) directly attributable cost savings or revenue increase	1	
		£10k–20k pa directly attributable cost savings or revenue increase	2	
		£21k–50k pa directly attributable cost savings or revenue increase	3	
		£51k–100k pa directly attributable cost savings or revenue increase	4	
		> £101k pa directly attributable cost savings or revenue increase	5	
2.	Will the data insight help your business to win or retain more clients?	No directly attributable client retention/acquisition	0	
		One directly attributable client retained/acquired	1	
		One or two directly attributable clients retained/acquired	2	
		Three to five directly attributable clients retained/acquired	3	
		Six to ten directly attributable clients retained/acquired	4	
		Eleven + directly attributable clients retained/acquired	5	

#	QUESTION		SCORE	RESULT
3.	Will the data insight give you a strategic advantage?	No strategic advantage	0	
		Small strategic advantage; eg to gain press coverage	1	
		Medium strategic advantage; eg to win an award	2	
		High strategic advantage; eg to win a high-profile client	3	
		Very high strategic advantage; eg to win many high-profile clients	4	
		Extremely high strategic advantage; eg to become the market leader	5	

I recommend that you assess every business need in this way; score them all and then prioritise the highest scoring ones for the first data projects. This will enable you to explain your rationale to all the stakeholders and make sure that they buy in to the prioritised list of data projects. This process can turn a sometimes subjective and contentious prioritisation process into an objective and business-goal-orientated process.

> Do you need a template or some help with this? Check out the Data Escalator Resources chapter at the end of the book.

If you use this approach, the defined revenue amounts and client volumes will need to be tailored for your business, and then validated and refined with your stakeholders, so that you get their buy-in to your methodology. I find this scoring approach is a pragmatic and objective way to prioritise business needs based on the commercial business value to your business.

You now understand the business needs, so your data project can be purposeful and targeted. You comprehend WHY people will benefit from using data. You know what they need to be able to see in the data. You get what they need to be able to do with the data. You've explored what they'll do differently when they see the data and what actions they'll take. You've even determined what they'll stop/start doing and what changes they'll make using the data. Can you see how this deep understanding of business needs will significantly improve your ability to deliver meaningful and valuable insight for your business?

Now you know the 'why', *you can focus on the 'how', 'when' and 'what'.*

REAL-WORLD EXAMPLE #1
A UK TRANSPORT PROVIDER SME

I will now share a business-needs-related case study with you to turn the theory described in this step into a practical, tactical example to bring it all to life. This will be using the example of a UK transport provider SME.

THE BUSINESS

A UK transport provider SME

THE DATA PROBLEM

This business is a high-growth, ambitious, scale-up SME with offices across the UK. With hundreds of employees and one core service offering, this business is technology led. Sales are made through multi-channel distribution with a focus on key account service activity. Customer transactions are high frequency, high volume and low value. Marketing activity is geo-targeted across the UK, through multiple digital and social media channels. Its data covers passengers, providers and business accounts, stored largely in one place. With on-premises information technology (IT) solutions, this truly is big data.

THE DATA OPPORTUNITY

- To derive actionable insight from the data

- To inform tactical business decisions on cost allocation

- To inform the business strategy during a high-growth phase

THE DATA PROCESS

1. Business requirements – A series of workshops were run with the operations, IT and marketing teams to understand the different business needs and business challenges.

2. Business review – The business model was reviewed to understand what business levers could be pulled when it comes to sales, marketing, products, pricing and channel activity.

3. Pilot project – A first project was identified as a proof of concept to explore what was possible with the data. This tested the ability to extract, combine and analyse big data across the business.

4. Prototype – A proof of concept was created to demonstrate the success of the pilot project and to facilitate key stakeholders visualising the data insight.

5. Business needs – Based on the prototype, more specific business needs were developed to a highly detailed level for each part of the business.

6. Business metrics – Brand-new business metrics were created. New ways to analyse customers were identified, such as passenger lifetime value and cost per acquisition. These were business specific and based on the way the organisation's business model worked.

7. Business-need prioritisation – As there were more business needs than resources available, the needs were categorised using the potential commercial value to the business and ranked in order of priority.

THE RESULT

The brand-new insight derived from the pilot project was used to inform the business plan and growth strategy for this business. Off the back of the pilot project, business-wide data requirements were developed further, using a multi-functional team, to fast-track data usage within the business.

THE STEP #1 BUSINESS NEEDS TIP

Wide engagement was required across the business to fully understand the business needs for this SME. So, the key for this project was to make certain that the data requirements were captured for the CEO, chief operating officer (COO), chief technology officer (CTO), chief financial officer (CFO) and the head of marketing. Without this wide-reaching and full understanding of the different business needs, the project wouldn't have delivered meaningful and actionable data insight for the business. However, the operations area was prioritised first, so this single business area served as a pilot before the requirements gathering was rolled out to the other business areas. This pilot, test and roll-out methodology worked well for this business.

LESSONS LEARNT #1
UNDERSTAND YOUR BUSINESS NEEDS

This book is based on my hands-on, practical experience of helping many businesses to understand the business needs behind their data opportunities, so I wanted to share some of the common mistakes I've seen and the lessons I've learnt, so you can ensure that you don't repeat the same errors in your business on Step #1 of the Data Escalator.

1. START SMALL

I see many businesses trying to tackle all of their data problems in one go, which can be overwhelming, overcomplicated, involve far too many people and end up being a false start. I recommend that you identify one part of your business, with a specific data challenge or opportunity, and start there first; this might be one product, one location or one department. Treat this first data project as a pilot or a test, so you can experiment, learn and share the results with the rest of your business before extending the data work to other business areas.

2. TIMEBOX YOUR PROJECT

A data project can be never-ending. There's always a new data source, more recent data, a new stakeholder or more feedback, and the project could continue for months or even years. So, define a specific timeline for your project right from the start; I recommend six weeks maximum for a prototype or proof of concept, for instance. This timebox will focus everyone's minds on the end goal and ensure you deliver something quickly and efficiently.

3. DON'T LET PERFECTION BE THE ENEMY OF GOOD

Sometimes you need 100% accuracy for a project to be successful, but most of the time you don't. So, don't hold back: state your assumptions clearly, show where data is incomplete, explain where there are gaps and deliver your data insight to your stakeholders. If version two is required to improve the accuracy or completeness of your data insight for your stakeholders to feel more confident, then do it. But make sure you share something quickly, rather than sharing nothing.

4. WIN HEARTS AND MINDS

For your first project, choose something that will excite and inspire your stakeholders. Perhaps there's a burning issue right now, something topical or a struggling part of the business. People often make decisions with their emotions first, then they use rationale to back up their decisions. We've seen data projects focus on business areas that are simply of no interest to their stakeholders, so they don't make any progress with the data within their organisation. Think about who your stakeholders are and what they care about, then deliver a project that they'll love.

5. NAIL DOWN THE SCOPE

You need to communicate clearly what's in scope for your project and what's not in scope. This is crucial to guaranteeing that, firstly, expectations are managed in advance and, secondly, if the scope changes, you can show unmistakeably what's changed and why. And the scope will change; it always does, without fail, on every project. So, nailing down the scope on day one and then managing changes to the scope are crucial to your project's success. This is the most common mistake I've experienced – and it can be costly. Literally.

You'll also learn your own lessons as your business-need experience grows. And you'll improve continually and grow in confidence as you do.

TASK #1 – DEFINE YOUR BUSINESS NEEDS AND BUSINESS LEVERS

Before you continue, your first task is to define the business needs and business levers for your first data project.

Take 10–20 minutes to start this now.

YOUR BUSINESS USERS	YOUR BUSINESS NEEDS	YOUR BUSINESS LEVERS
Who are they? *What department are they in?* *What motivates them?*	*What do they want to know?* *What insight do they need?* *What hypotheses, assumptions or urban myths do they have?*	*What can your business users do with the potential data insight that you'll generate for them?* *What could your business users start/stop/change in the business?* *How much money could your business users make or save for the business?* *How many clients could your business users win or retain for the business?* *Could your business users create a new strategic advantage?*
	Your Business	

Your Business		

You can develop this further in the coming days, weeks and months of your data project.

Do you need a template or some help with this? Check out the Data Escalator Resources chapter at the end of the book.

STEP #2

DEFINE YOUR
DATA STRATEGY

*If you don't know where you're going, you'll
never get there*

STEP #2 – DEFINE YOUR DATA STRATEGY

Do you have a data strategy? Or, in simpler terms, do you know what you want to achieve with data for your business? For instance, do you know what your vision is, what your objectives are, what the outputs will be, what your goals are, what resources you need, what technology you'll use, how much it will cost, what the risks are and so on. If not, you're likely to end up doing nothing. Or, even worse, you're likely to deliver a range of tactical, isolated, disconnected things with your data, which could potentially make your data challenge even more complex to solve in future. Plus, there's a risk that you could introduce more risks and costs into your business as a result of not thinking things through properly.

Don't worry if you don't have a data strategy – you're not alone. Most businesses don't have a data strategy unless they have a chief data officer or head of data, which is a luxury largely afforded to large organisations only, not your everyday SME. So, let's create a data strategy now…

Why use data?

The first question to be prepared for when creating a data strategy is why use data at all? Clearly, as you're taking the time to read this book, you get it. But do your stakeholders, board, leadership team, employees or customers? Don't assume that everyone believes in the value of data. You need to take the time to explain why data is a massively valuable business asset. Here are some reasons to help you do this:

Reason 1 – Data is objective

It's factual, removes guesswork, eradicates subjectivity and diminishes personal preferences. The days of making decisions based on whoever shouts the loudest should be over. Data is the tool you can use to ensure business decisions are made objectively, factually and in an informed way.

Reason 2 – Data could tell you new things about your business

You could uncover new patterns and trends; prove or disprove business hypotheses or urban myths; test previously held assumptions; or replace estimates or historical figures with facts.

Reason 3 – Data is a potential business asset

Big businesses are valuing data so highly that it's being added to their balance sheets. Data is making or will make businesses more money. And who doesn't want to make more money for their business?

So, once you've convinced people that using data is a source of business value, it's down to defining the data strategy.

Where to start

There are three ways to start defining your business's data strategy:

1. **Top-down** – Where you use the business strategy to inform the data strategy, so that the data strategy becomes a sub-component of the business strategy.

2. **Bottom-up** – Where data insight is used to inform the creation of a data strategy and this then informs the business strategy.

3. **Hybrid** – Where you use a combination of a top-down and bottom-up approach for data strategy development.

Each of these methods is a good way to build a data strategy, so let's explore every one in turn.

Top-down data strategy development

A top-down data strategy starts with your business strategy. Hence, the first action is to review your business-strategy document. But what if you don't have a business strategy yet? Or if you do, perhaps it's unavailable, incomplete or out of date? This is where you can use a business strategy workshop to gain strategic input from your business leaders instead.

The questions you'll want to ask your business leaders are as follows:

a. *What's the primary business priority?*

The answer could be one of these:

✓ Acquisition – winning X more clients or £X revenue next year

✓ Retention – reducing attrition from X% to Y%

✓ Expansion – launching into X more markets with Y more products

b. *What are the core metrics or key performance indicators (KPIs) you use to measure performance?*

The answer could include one or more of these:

✓ Financial – revenue, cost and/or profit

✓ Customer – volume, lifetime value, retention and/or satisfaction

✓ Sales – leads, conversion rates and/or new-client volumes

✓ Marketing – response rates, engagement and/or brand awareness

✓ People – attrition rate, performance, absence and/or engagement

✓ Service – SLAs, efficiency, errors and/or downtime

c. *Who are your target customers?*

The answer could include specifying one or more of these:

✓ Type – individuals and/or businesses

✓ Location

✓ Business size and/or sector

✓ Demographics

✓ Socioeconomic factors

✓ Characteristics

✓ Needs

✓ Behaviours

d. *Where are you performing well and not well?*

The answer could vary by one or more of these:

✓ Location

✓ Product

✓ Department

✓ Customer segment

✓ Channel

e. *What are the critical success factors for data within your business?*

The answer could include one or more of these:

✓ Data security

✓ Compliance

✓ Regulation

✓ Governance

✓ Brand and values

✓ Reporting specifications

✓ Creating a competitive advantage

✓ Delivering within a defined timescale

✓ Solving a defined problem first

This top-down approach will help you to see where data can be used to support your business strategy, so that your data strategy can be complementary and aligned to it. Your data strategy NEEDS to power your business strategy to be successful, both in terms of your data outputs and politically; your stakeholders need to see data as part of the solution for business growth, and not as an isolated or separate business task. It's imperative that you have the buy-in of your senior leadership team right from the start.

Bottom-up data strategy development

A bottom-up data strategy starts with the data, which is then used to inform the business strategy. Hence, this starts with the data and the insight that already exists within your business. To collate this data and insight, you'll probably need to speak to different people within your business, as different people often hold different parts of the data puzzle. This could include your data team (if you have one), customer service team, finance team, sales team, marketing team and so on. You'll need to ask each of them about the data and the insight they have derived from the data in their business area; this needs to include asking them what they don't know.

Here are some examples of how the answers are likely to vary significantly depending on whom you speak to. So, make sure you speak to all the core business areas.

BUSINESS AREA	WHAT YOU KNOW	WHAT YOU DON'T KNOW
Customer Services	How many customers we have Who calls us the most Who complains the most What are the variations by hour/day of the week	How customers have changed over time Who our high-value customers are Which clients are good/bad payers Who attends our events
Finance	How much revenue we receive How much we spend Which clients are good/bad payers What the variations by product/location are	What revenue will be next month/year What the cost per acquisition is How profitable each customer is How efficient our people are

BUSINESS AREA	WHAT YOU KNOW	WHAT YOU DON'T KNOW
Sales	Number of leads generated Lead-to-sales conversion rate Number of new clients every month How satisfied customers are	How profitable each customer is How long customers stay with us Who engages with marketing activity Who attends our events
Marketing	How we segment our customers How many customers engage with us How many customers attend events How many leads we generate	What the return on investment (ROI) is for marketing activity What our cost per acquisition is Who our highest-value customers are How many leads convert to sales
Human Resources	How many staff we have How much we pay people How many sick days employees take Which employees are poor performers	Which employees generate the most sales Which employees offer great service Which employees engage with the board Which employees might resign

This data can be used to inform the data strategy and, ultimately, the business strategy, as it will show you the current facts and figures available across the business, as well as the gaps and potential data opportunities.

Hybrid data strategy development

This is a combination of the top-down and bottom-up approaches to data strategy development, and it's our recommended methodology. The top-down approach will make sure that you're aligned to the business strategy and to your strategic business requirements. The bottom-up approach will ensure that you don't duplicate or ignore what's already been done.

Which one should you do first? That depends on your business and your role. If you believe that you'll receive good engagement across the business, then start with the bottom-up approach and use the information you gain to run a top-down data strategy workshop with your business leaders; this will mean that you'll know what you're talking about, which will inspire confidence in your ability to implement the data strategy.

If, however, you think you need buy-in from senior leadership in order to be able to fully engage all business areas for the bottom-up approach, you'll need to start with the top-down approach. Once you have senior leadership commitment, you'll then have a mandate to run the bottom-up approach across all business areas.

In both cases, your data strategy should evolve as you bring in both the top-down and bottom-up components. Regular iterations of developing your data strategy are the key, so keep an open mind throughout this process and try not to jump to conclusions early.

Data skills assessment

Most businesses have limited data skills, knowledge and experience in-house, so performing a data skills assessment is a good way to determine where you are currently and where you want to get to.

When running a data skills assessment, it's worth thinking about who to include within the scope of your assessment. For instance, some businesses have a centralised data team, so you could focus entirely on that team. But many businesses have different data-related roles in various teams, where multiple people are working with data in one way, shape or form – such as an analyst in finance, a business intelligence (BI) developer in customer services, a marketing data manager, and a variety of data-related roles in the IT department. Plus, job titles are sometimes not self-explanatory when it comes to data: a project manager or marketing manager might be doing a lot of work with data, for example. Hence, it's important to consider the scope of your data skills assessment to make sure that you rate your business's data skills accurately.

Once you've defined which roles and people are in scope for your data skills assessment, you can choose to assess the skills either at a business level or at an individual level.

Here's an example of a skills assessment at the business level:

DATA AREA	DATA SKILLS	SCORE OUT OF 10	
		TODAY	TARGET
Data consultancy	Business knowledge, commercial skills and facilitation		
Data engineering	Architecture and design		
	Extract, transform and load (ETL); Python; and SQL		
Data analysis	Analytics and statistics		
Data science	ML and advanced statistics		
	Predictive models and R		
Data visualisation	Power BI, Tableau, design skills and insight generation		
	User-interface development and HTML		

A business-level data skills assessment is a useful way to rate your business at present and set your business a target for future data skills levels.

You can also take a similar approach to assess data skills at an individual team-member level, where you want to score individual data skills within your business. Here's an example:

DATA AREA	DATA SKILLS	SCORE OUT OF 10		
		Jane	Eva	Amir
Data consultancy	Business knowledge, commercial skills and facilitation	9	3	0
Data engineering	Architecture and design	7	9	0
	ETL, Python and SQL	0	10	7
Data analysis	Analytics and statistics	0	3	9
Data science	ML and advanced statistics	0	0	8
	Predictive models and R	0	0	8
Data visualisation	Power BI, Tableau, design skills and insight	5	5	5
	User-interface development and HTML	7	7	0

In both types of data skills assessment, the scores of 0 to 10 can either be subjective or defined using a set scoring model. If you want to define a scoring model, you could use an approach like this:

0   No experience at all

2   Minimal experience

4   Some experience, but no training

6   Regular experience and trained to beginner level

8   Frequent and extensive experience, and trained to an advanced level

10   Highly experienced and well trained; they could run a training course themselves

So long as you're consistent with your scoring methodology over time, and providing it gives you room to score people as their skills advance, then this process can be tailored for your organisation.

Once you've completed your data skills assessment, you can consider where you'd like your data skills to be within the next year, five years or time period of your choice. This will give you today's score vs your target score, which will be a useful goal for you to add to your data strategy.

Do you need some help with this? Check out the Data Escalator Resources chapter at the end of the book.

Data maturity assessment

You can now consider where your business is currently on a data maturity curve:

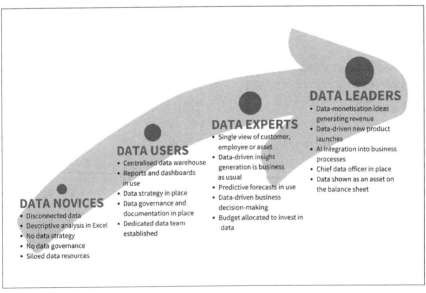

Figure 1: The data maturity curve

Data novices tend to be either established businesses or scale-up businesses:

- Established businesses that have grown beyond their original data architecture over the years and are now at the point where they need to invest in data to support their larger business and future-growth plans. They're likely to see data as a problem because different people are quoting different numbers, and there's no single version of the truth within the business. They may also feel vulnerable regarding how robust and secure their data is, as well as being concerned if they're compliant with data regulations.

- Scale-up businesses that have grown fast, and the data architecture now needs to catch up to ensure that their data is robust, secure and compliant. They're likely to see data as an opportunity if they can get it right – an opportunity to make more money and power their business growth. It's an area for investment.

Data users tend to be businesses that have identified that data is either a problem or an opportunity, and they've started on the journey to fix it. They're likely to have bought licences for third-party data tools, created a data warehouse, recruited a team of people to look after data, and started improving their data governance and documentation. Data will be mentioned in their business plans. Reports and dashboards will be shared across the business.

Data experts tend to be businesses that have invested significantly in data through people, training, tools and strategic projects. They're likely to have a data director or head of data, who is empowered with a decent-sized team, a budget and a training schedule, and with cutting-edge AI and ML tools at their disposal. Data will be a core part of their business strategy, customer offering and shareholder updates. Data-driven analytics will be used routinely across the business to inform business decisions.

Data leaders tend to be businesses that are presenting at data conferences; launching data-driven, market-leading services for customers; and widely regarded as global data innovators. They're likely to have a chief data officer or another dedicated data role on the senior leadership team. Data will be a core part of shareholder updates and innovation development.

So, where is your business on the data-maturity curve right now? In my experience, most businesses are low down on the maturity curve and moving from being data novices to becoming data users through the creation of automated data reports and dashboards. Some businesses are moving from being data users to becoming data experts through the creation of a single view of customers and using predictive tools. Data leaders tend to be the minority of businesses that have invested heavily in data in the last decade or brand-new start-ups that have been built with a data ethos right from the start.

Now you can consider where you'd like your business to move to on the data-maturity curve within the next year, five years or time period of your choice. Your decision needs to be based on what's realistic for your business. Consider where you are just now, how much your business is willing to invest, how high data is on your priority list, how much support there is from the senior leadership team, and what timeframe you want to focus on. This will give you another goal to add to your data strategy, and a target for your stakeholders.

Data strategy creation

What's a data strategy? Is it a 50-page document? Or a 10-slide presentation? It could be either; there is no one-size-fits-all data strategy, as it needs to be tailored for your business. However, there are some core areas that should be included within your data strategy:

* **Objective**
  * What's the primary purpose of this data strategy?
  * How does the data strategy help the company to achieve the business objectives?
  * Are you maintaining, evolving or transforming what you do currently?

- Is there a metric or KPI that you want to achieve?

* **Vision**

  - What does 'good' look like?
  - What's the ultimate end goal for the data strategy in one, five or 10 years?
  - How will the business be improved as a result of this data strategy?
  - Where are you on the data maturity curve, and where would you like to get to?

* **Scope**

  - What's in and out of scope?
  - Does this data strategy cover all locations, products and departments?
  - What data sources are included across your business areas, tools and platforms?
  - Is there a limit on what data will be included?

* **Priorities**

  - What are the quick wins?
  - What are you doing first, second and third?
  - Why have these areas been prioritised?
  - Why have other areas been de-prioritised?

* **Governance**

  - How will you comply with legal requirements and regulations?
  - How will you handle data security?
  - How will your data strategy support your brand and values?
  - What documentation and user guides will you produce?

* **Resources**

  - How will your data skills change?
  - Will you use in-house resources or external resources?
  - Will you use your current team or recruit new people?
  - What training and upskilling will be required?

* **Budget**

  - What are the costs over time?
  - What are the costs for resources, third-party tools, licences, training, etc.?
  - Are there any cost savings?
  - Are there any cost uncertainties?

* **Timeline**

  - What tasks will be required?
  - Who will do the tasks?
  - When will they do the tasks?
  - Is there any contingency built in?

* **Risks**

  - Are there any compliance risks?
  - Are there any commercial risks?
  - Are there any people-related risks?
  - Are there any issues that could impact the successful delivery of the data strategy?

As you can see, your data strategy requires significant effort, research, preparation and thought. Whilst your data strategy could be created in a day, the knowledge and thinking could take you some time to work through, both individually and with your stakeholders.

I love a one-page data strategy, because if you can't explain your data strategy on a page, you'll never be able to explain it to your board, leadership team or key stakeholders. Whilst there will be a lot of detailed content that sits behind your one-page data strategy, I highly recommend that you create one for situations where you have limited time with key decision-makers.

Being a data leader

Creating a data strategy is just the start. It's just a document or set of slides until you get your business to really buy into it. This requires you to lead your business: to become the data leader, to advocate the use of data as a business asset and to lead the change.

So how can you inspire, influence and lead your business to support your data strategy?

a. Identify a fellow advocate

Find someone who will support you, champion data and influence the change. Start with one member of your leadership team, perhaps your CTO, who can support you with the technology angle; or your chief commercial officer (CCO) or sales director, who will focus on the commercial value of data. Work in partnership with them to develop a strategy to win the hearts and minds of the other members of the leadership team.

b. Start with a showcase project

Focus on one business area first, deliver a data-led business benefit quickly and use this to show other parts of the business what the potential opportunities are. Choose a project that's topical and challenging but where you can deliver a data solution within six weeks. You don't want a project that could last for months, otherwise you won't be able to make an immediate impact. You want to demonstrate a quick win to show that data can add value to your business today.

c. Business first, data second

Prioritise your data strategy based on business needs, and talk in the language of your business. Focus on the business's problems and concerns first. Show that data is part of the solution. Explain how data can help the business to achieve its objectives quickly, cheaply or easily. Business is the priority – data is the answer.

d. Make data simple

Don't dazzle people with data jargon. Don't make data complicated. Don't focus on the technological, coding or statistical details, unless they ask about them specifically. Otherwise, you risk losing their attention and, ultimately, their trust. If you can't make data simple for them, you'll look like you don't know what you're talking about.

These skills take practise and may require some trial and error. But don't give up. If your first showcase project or data-strategy meeting doesn't work, then learn from your mistakes, come back and try again.

By defining your data strategy, you'll know what you want to achieve with data for your business. You'll be able to share your vision, show your objectives, list the planned outputs, target specified KPIs, list your resource requirements, outline your budget and explain the risks to your business. Can you see how this clarity will significantly improve your ability to win the hearts and minds of your leadership team and stakeholders?

Now you know where you're going, *you're much more likely to get there.*

REAL-WORLD EXAMPLE #2
A GLOBAL FINANCIAL SERVICES CORPORATION

Creating a data strategy for a business from scratch for the first time can be challenging. So, to inspire you, I'm going to detail a data-strategy-related case study for you to transform the concepts I've explained thus far into a concrete example. This time it relates to a global financial services corporation.

THE BUSINESS

A global financial services corporation

THE DATA PROBLEM

This corporation is massive. They have global offices, many functional departments and thousands of employees. With multiple product suites and multi-currency pricing, their business offering is diverse. Like many global corporations, they focus on key account sales activity, and they have networks of intermediaries for distribution and supply chains. They run high-frequency marketing campaigns across global regions, and they have a strong brand presence. Their data includes information on products, customers and financials, which is stored largely in two core databases. The business is complicated as a result of decades of business history and legacy technology systems from past mergers and acquisitions. This is a complex business structure with a ton of data.

THE DATA OPPORTUNITY

- To find the golden nuggets in the data
- To tell the organisation something new about the business by analysing data in new ways

- To generate brand-new insight for the organisation using data

THE DATA PROCESS

1. Strategy selection – A bottom-up strategy development approach was selected, as the work originated from the data team, which had access to most of the business data within the organisation.

2. Business-area engagement – The strategy, sales and marketing teams were engaged to determine their current data understanding and data gaps.

3. Pilot project – A first project was selected as a test case to explore what was possible with the data. This tested the ability to extract, combine and analyse the data across the business.

4. Prototype – A proof of concept was created to demonstrate the success of the pilot project and to visualise the data insight to the key stakeholders.

5. Data strategy – Based on the results of the pilot project, a data strategy was created for the business, which shared the current data-skills assessment, data-maturity assessment and bottom-up data insight with the board.

THE RESULT

Brand-new insight, derived from the pilot project, was shared with the leadership team. This informed the creation and approval of the organisation's data strategy. In turn, this resulted in more money being invested in data, in the form of people and budgets for future data projects.

THE STEP #2 DATA STRATEGY TIP

For this organisation, the key was to start with a pilot project and keep it below the radar. The small project group worked quietly, and the results were only shared when the team had confidence in the outcome. This enabled expectations to be managed and the risk of project failure to be minimised. The launch of the data solution was a surprise to the members of the organisation, and it revealed the results of work that they didn't even know was happening within the business. This approach worked for this specific global financial services corporation due to its culture, and it played a key role in achieving board-level support for both the data strategy and future data projects.

LESSONS LEARNT #2
DEFINE YOUR DATA STRATEGY

Defining data strategy is another area in which I have much practical experience of assisting many businesses. I've made lots of mistakes and learnt the hard way, so I wanted to share my experiences with you in the hope that you won't fall foul of similar mistakes in your business on Step #2 of the Data Escalator.

1. BE PRAGMATIC

You could spend months creating the perfect data strategy, but deliver nothing. Don't. You'll not be judged on having the perfect data-strategy document, but you'll be judged on the successful delivery of data outputs. So, create version one of your data strategy, start delivering data solutions and refine your data strategy as you go. This way, you can aim for the right balance between strategic thinking and pragmatic, results-orientated delivery.

2. COMPLEMENT THE BUSINESS STRATEGY

Make certain that your data strategy aligns with your business strategy, so it's part of the solution. Whatever you do, don't position data as being something different or separate to the rest of your business. Data needs to be at the core of your business, it needs to help your business grow and it needs to be championed by your leadership team. It can't be delegated or dealt with in silos, otherwise your data strategy will fail. A joined-up approach is critical to the success of your data strategy.

3. ITERATE, ITERATE, ITERATE

The hybrid data strategy development approach is built on iteration, so don't forget to review your data strategy regularly as your data projects prove or disprove data hypotheses within your business, and as you discover new patterns and trends. If you're doing a great job, your data strategy will be evolving all the time. Treat it as the living, breathing, evolving documentation of your strategic data journey. Not a once-a-year tick-box task.

4. ASK FOR HELP

Creating a new data strategy for any business is hard. The larger the business, the harder it is. You'll need help to succeed. So, ask for it – from internal stakeholders and colleagues who you need to get on side, and from external data experts who have done it all before and can share their experiences with you. Whenever you're feeling defeated, you're feeling overwhelmed or you can't see the wood for the trees, ask for help.

5. BE PREPARED FOR CHALLENGES

Be warned that creating a business-wide data strategy is not for the faint-hearted. You'll encounter resistance when you're creating a data strategy. Some people will feel threatened that you're going to use data against them. Others will feel it's their job and you're treading on their toes. Data cuts across a business. Yet most businesses operate in silos, otherwise known as departments, teams and functions. Your project needs to break down the silos – and breaking down silos is tough! Be prepared for this process to be challenging, and trust that you're doing the right thing for the business.

You'll also learn your own lessons as your data strategy evolves, and you'll improve continually and grow in confidence as you do.

TASK #2 – DEFINE YOUR DATA STRATEGY

Before you continue, your second task is to share some high-level thoughts on the likely top-down and bottom-up inputs in your business, and then take a view on how you'd approach your hybrid data strategy development.

Take 10–20 minutes to start this now.

TOP-DOWN INPUTS	BOTTOM-UP INPUTS	HYBRID
What are your business objectives? *What are your business priorities?*	*What data facts do you know already?* *What business statistics get reported today?*	*Where are you on the data-maturity curve?* *What do you expect your data priorities to be?*
Your Business		

Your Business		

You can develop this further in the coming days, weeks and months, depending on the requirements for your business.

Do you need a template or some help with this? Check out the Data Escalator Resources chapter at the end of the book.

STEP #3

MAP YOUR DATA SOURCES

*If you don't know what data is available,
you'll miss the good stuff*

STEP #3 – MAP YOUR DATA SOURCES

Do you know what data you have available to play with at the moment? Think about all the databases being used within your business currently, the third-party tools and platforms you use, the legacy systems you have, and the external data you buy in. In any business, even a small business, you're likely to have multiple data sources in multiple locations. In my experience, SME businesses usually have 10–20 data sources.

If you don't explore all of your data sources first, before getting started, you're likely to miss out on valuable data insight. Hence, it's important to take the time to identify, review and map all the data sources across your business, so you can plan your data project.

Identifying data sources

Data can come from different sources, in different formats, from all parts of your business. Think about the data concerning your customers, people, finances, assets, performance, products, marketing and more. Think about the data you own, the data you process and the data you acquire. Think about databases, spreadsheets, user interfaces, recordings, images, third-party tools and so on. With so many types of data in so many locations, it's easy to miss some. (There's a checklist for you on the following page.)

It's worth thinking about the benefits of combining data sources together, including the following:

✓ If you combine customer data with financial data, you can calculate the revenue per client

✓ If you combine marketing data with sales data, you can calculate the cost per client acquisition

Here's a checklist for you to start exploring your existing data sources:

FUNCTION	DATA SOURCES	CHECKLIST
Finance	Accounting tools Invoicing data Accounts payable data Purchasing data Tax-reporting tool Expense logs	
Customer Services	Call centre platform Customer services tools Customer-survey tool Call-recording tool Point-of-sale tool Footfall-tracking tool	
Sales	Lead-generation tool Sales-pipeline tool Bids-and-tenders tool Time-management tool Proposal tool	
Marketing	Email tool Website analytics E-commerce platform Social media platform Social media monitoring tool Public relations monitoring tool Event-management tool Webinar/online-meeting tool Advertising platform	
Partners	Distributor tool Supplier tool Retailer tool Intermediary platform	

FUNCTION	DATA SOURCES	CHECKLIST
People	HR management system Payroll tool Employee benefits platform Employee share scheme Recruitment tool Performance-management tool Holiday/absence-tracking tool Employee-assistance platform	
IT	On-premises database Cloud database Helpdesk tool Hardware audit Telecommunications platform Security platform	
Clients	CRM database Client data provided to your business to deliver their product(s)/service(s)	
External	Market data Government data Local council / local authority data Weather data Demographic data Prospect lists	

Plus, there are many more, depending on your business type, sector, coverage, scale, etc. So you should consider this checklist as your starting point, not your end point.

Combining data sources together (from the tick-bullet suggestions on page 68) can also deliver valuable insight, so study your data sources carefully at this stage, and go far and wide.

Exploring different data types

When exploring your data, it's important to consider data in all its forms, so you don't miss out on any opportunities. Let's look at three different data types:

1. **Internal vs external data**

2. **Structured vs unstructured data**

3. **Data vs big data**

1. Internal vs external data

Internal data is that which is owned, stored or processed within your business. This could be data owned by your business or data owned by someone else but processed by your business.

Internal data could include one or more of these:

- Data on your business that is stored in your databases
- Data in third-party tools that is used by your business
- Data sent to your business by your clients, partners, distributors, retailers or suppliers

Whereas, external data is sourced from a third party outside your organisation. This could be data purchased by your business or publicly available data acquired by your business.

External data could include one or more of these:

- Market data; eg interest rates
- Government data; eg unemployment rates
- Local council / local authority data; eg the number of residents
- Weather data; eg data from the Met Office

- Demographic data; eg Acorn data from CACI
- Prospect lists

External data can be derived from many different public and private sources; you could start with a Google search. Do your research to check you're using accurate, legal and compliant data.

2. Structured vs unstructured data

Structured data is what you'd consider to be 'normal' data, as it easily fits into data fields and spreadsheets. Often categorised as quantitative data, structured data includes the following:

- Numbers
- Volumes
- Financials
- Addresses
- Postcodes
- Ratings
- Scores

Structured data is easy to analyse, categorise and process.

Whereas, unstructured data is the most common type of data and is highly variable in nature and content. Often categorised as qualitative data, unstructured data includes the following:

- Text
- Audio
- Video
- Imagery

- Commentary
- Feedback
- Descriptions

Unstructured data is harder to analyse, categorise and process because this can't be done in a simple spreadsheet, but it needs more complex and advanced analytical methods, which we'll explore in Step #6 when we talk about analysing your data.

3. Data vs big data

You've probably heard the term 'big data' – it's a term that's bandied around often. Yet there isn't a standard definition for what big data is. There's no set number of terabytes (TB) of data, for instance, that we can neatly fit big data into.

However, you can test if you have big data by considering the five Vs:

1. **Volume** – How much data do you have? Can you open it in Excel? If so, then it's small. Do you need a supercomputer? If so, then it's big.

2. **Variety** – Is everything in a neat table of structured numbers? Or do you have loads of unstructured data from social media, audio recordings and imagery? Unstructured data is 'bigger' than structured data as it's harder to categorise and file.

3. **Veracity** – Can you trust your data? Do you know if it's a reliable data source with consistent data-processing methods? If not, you may need more analysis. We can consider this data to be complex and therefore big.

4. **Velocity** – Are you collecting data every year, such as for financial services policies? It's probably small. Or are you collecting data every second or micro-second, such as from a social media platform? It's probably big.

5. **Value** – Could the data be sliced and diced in many different ways to identify patterns and trends that you couldn't even anticipate? If so, it could be considered to be big in terms of value.

If you're collecting data every second, your data is too big to process on a laptop and/or if you need a coder to analyse it, then it's probably big data. Just by looking at a business from a distance, you can probably guess that they have big data if they collect data every second or micro-second. Examples include social media businesses with user-generated content, real-time sensor businesses and transport/retail businesses with 24/7 transactions.

But most data isn't big, it's small data. Or just data. If you're collecting data monthly or annually, and your data is normally analysed in Excel or spreadsheets, it's probably small. Again, just by considering a business from afar, you can probably guess that they have small (or not big) data if they collect data daily, monthly or annually. Examples include financial services businesses with annual policies, travel companies with one-off holiday bookings and market research companies with monthly surveys.

Whether your data is internal or external, structured or unstructured, or big or small, it's still valuable. Most businesses have a mix of all these data types.

Creating a data catalogue

Most data is disparate and disconnected, so the best way to feel more in control of your data is to list of all your data sources in one place. You can do this by creating a data catalogue for your business. This is a record of all your data sources, where they are, what they contain, how big they are and who's responsible for them.

Here are the fields you should consider for your data catalogue:

- ✓ Data source name; eg customer database
- ✓ Primary purpose of the database; eg customer management
- ✓ Who is accountable for the data source within the business; eg the business owner
- ✓ Who is responsible for managing the data source within the business; eg the technology team

✓ Data source type; eg third-party platform

✓ Data source location; eg cloud-hosted or on-site

✓ Data source security; eg access controls and backups

✓ Data size; eg megabytes (MB) or TB

✓ Data type; eg structured or external

✓ Data source start date; eg 1 April 2010

Here's a sample data catalogue:

DATA SOURCE	PURPOSE	OWNER (accountable)	MANAGER (responsible)	TYPE	LOCATION	SECURITY	SIZE	DATA	START DATE
Customer	Contact records	Chief marketing officer (CMO)	Sales director	Salesforce	Cloud	Restricted access	100 MB	Structured	1 April 2010
Operations	Worksites	COO	Site manager	In-house database	On premises	Open access	2 TB	Unstructured	1 April 2010

Despite this being a simple task, most businesses don't have a data catalogue. But taking the time to create your data catalogue will save you loads of time later on down the line. You'll have all your data sources listed in one place, which can inform your data strategy, be used across your business and fast-track your future data projects. It's important to review it regularly, update the relevant fields when things change, and add new data sources as they come into your business.

Do you need a template or some help with this? Check out the Data Escalator Resources chapter at the end of the book.

Building a data dictionary

Now you have a data catalogue, you can describe the data within these data sources in the form of a data dictionary. This is a list of all your data fields, what they are, what format they're in and their range. This process will ensure that your data is used in the right way and not misinterpreted. Data field names are not always self-explanatory, so a data dictionary will help to guarantee that you're extracting the right data field and using it in the way it was intended.

For each data source, you should consider the following for your data dictionary:

- ✓ List all data fields within each data source

- ✓ Identify the unique identifier in each data source; ie the field that is never duplicated and can be used to identify an individual record

- ✓ Describe the expected content in each data field; ie provide a description

- ✓ Define the expected format of the data in each data field; eg date, number or currency

- ✓ Define the expected range of data in each data field; eg minimum and maximum values

Here's a sample data dictionary:

DATA SOURCE	DATA FIELD	UNIQUE IDENTIFIER	CONTENT	FORMAT	MIN	MAX
Customer database	Customer ID	Yes	ID for every business client	Nine-digit number	0	999999999
	Customer name	No	Name of business	Text	String > 1	String < 200

Again, most businesses don't have a data dictionary. However, taking the time to create your data dictionary will save you loads of time later on down the line. You'll have all your data fields listed in one place, which can fast-track the data extraction process on your future data projects. It's important to review it regularly, update fields when things change, and add new data sources and fields as they come into your business.

Creating a data dictionary is a large task for many businesses, as you could have hundreds of data fields. Start with your priority data sources first, then build it out as you run future data projects. It's well worth the effort, and the task will only get harder as your business grows and the number of data fields increase, so start now.

You now know what data you have available at the moment to play with in your business, the third-party tools and platform you use, the legacy systems you have, the external data you buy in, and the multiple data sources you have in multiple locations across your business. Can you see how important it is to take the time to identify, review and map all data sources across your business to inform your data project?

Now you know what data is available, *you can include the good stuff.*

REAL-WORLD EXAMPLE #3
A REGIONAL CHAMBER OF COMMERCE

This third example is a data-source-mapping case study, which showcases a genuine business situation involving the theories on data mapping described in this step, to facilitate your understanding. This instance uses a regional chamber of commerce and its disparate, disconnected data sources as an illustration.

THE BUSINESS

A regional chamber of commerce.

THE DATA PROBLEM

This organisation is a not-for-profit company. It is a membership business representing thousands of organisations, and it has regional offices and a headquarters culture. With hundreds of employees presenting multiple service offerings, this organisation is diverse. There are multi-channel sales routes, multiple revenue sources and multiple pricing options. Its data covers business customers, product sales and marketing activity. Data is sourced from a variety of both internal and external sources in a range of formats and in multiple systems. Disparate, disconnected data is the challenge for this organisation.

THE DATA OPPORTUNITY

- To combine multiple data sources together for the first time
- To showcase the company's reach
- To inform tactical business decisions on sales and marketing activity

THE DATA PROCESS

1. Business requirements – A workshop was run with the leadership team to understand and prioritise their business requirements.

2. Data source review – The data was stored in multiple places, in multiple formats and in multiple ways; there were more than 20 individual data sources.

3. Data categorisation – The data was identified as being internal vs external and structured vs unstructured.

4. Data catalogue – The 20+ data sources were listed and explained in one place for the first time.

5. Data map – The 20+ data sources were visualised in one place for the first time, showing how the data could be combined, merged and analysed.

THE RESULT

Using the enhanced understanding of the data sources, brand-new dashboards were developed to show the company's scale, reach, and variety of members, products, services and performance – all in one place for the first time. A series of follow-up data projects were implemented across the business too.

THE STEP #3 DATA MAPPING TIP

For this business, once all 20+ data sources had been reviewed, they were drawn on a massive piece of paper that was used to plan how the data would be connected across these data sources. This visual method was helpful for planning the data-matching processes. Standing back and doing this mapping work at the start ensured that the data-processing work was planned, streamlined and transparent to everyone on the project team.

LESSONS LEARNT #3
MAP YOUR DATA SOURCES

There are many pitfalls with respect to businesses mapping their data sources. Therefore, once again, I will detail many of the common mistakes I've seen and the lessons I've learnt, so you can check that you don't duplicate those mistakes in your business on Step #3 of the Data Escalator.

1. DOCUMENT YOUR DATA SOURCES

Most businesses I've spoken to don't have a data catalogue or data dictionary. This means that their data can feel even more disparate, disconnected and complex than it is. Therefore, please don't miss this step on the Data Escalator. Documenting your data sources will enable you to feel in control of your data, communicate to your stakeholders more clearly and identify new data opportunities for your business.

2. BREAK DOWN THE SILOS

Most businesses have separate departments, functions, roles, responsibilities, budgets and goals to facilitate the business working efficiently. However, these divisions frequently mean that everyone sees just their part of the data puzzle, not the whole. This often means that data sources are owned and managed by a variety of people within a business; for instance, marketing will own the marketing data tools, finance will own the financial data tools, and so on. For your data-mapping work to be successful, you need to work across all these divisions within your business to create one business view of your data sources. So, don't let the silos get in your way – involve everyone.

3. DON'T FORGET UNSTRUCTURED DATA

Most projects focus on structured data because it's readily available and easier to analyse. For some projects, that might be the right thing to do, but for other projects, you might be missing out on valuable insight by excluding unstructured data. Whilst it's harder to analyse, unstructured data can bring considerable value to a project if the purpose of the project makes it relevant.

4. DON'T FORGET EXTERNAL DATA

Similarly, most projects focus on internal data because it's immediately available and straightforward to access. However, you might be missing out on crucial insight and identifying interesting patterns and trends by excluding external data. Whilst it's harder to access, external data can bring serious value to a project if it's relevant to the objectives of your project.

5. DON'T FOCUS ON THE GAPS

Most businesses think their data is the worst of any business in the world as all they can see are the gaps and inconsistencies. Nonetheless, it's never as bad as they fear. Yes, there will be gaps, and, yes, there will be incomplete data fields, but this is normal. Never have I ever seen a project with 100% perfect data. It doesn't exist. So, you should focus on what you've got, rather than what you don't have.

You'll also learn your own lessons as your data-mapping work evolves, and you'll improve continually and grow in confidence as you do.

TASK #3 – CREATE YOUR DATA CATALOGUE

Before you continue, your next task is to create a data catalogue.

Take 10–20 minutes to start this now.

DATA SOURCE	PURPOSE	OWNER (accountable)	MANAGER (responsible)	TYPE	LOCATION	SECURITY	SIZE	DATA	START DATE
Name	What's it for?	Who's accountable?	Who's responsible?	eg SQL	eg cloud	eg restricted access	MB/ TB	eg structured	When was it set up?

You can develop this further in the coming days, weeks and months of your data project.

Do you need a template or some help with this? Check out the Data Escalator Resources chapter at the end of the book.

STEP #4

CONNECT YOUR DATA

If you don't know where the dots are, you'll never join them up

STEP #4 – CONNECT YOUR DATA

Now you need to connect all your selected data sources together, so that you can start to do interesting things with your data. Most data projects will have multiple data sources, and they're often disconnected and disparate. If you leave them disconnected, you'll only be able to analyse them in isolation, which could create valuable insight in isolation. However, by connecting the data sources so that they can be analysed together in combination, there is far more potential for you to generate more significant and more valuable insight.

Think about being able to combine your financial data with your customer data to understand profit per customer or customer value. Think about connecting your sales data with your marketing data to understand cost per acquisition and ROI. If you don't connect the data, you'll never be able to generate cross-departmental business insight.

Data connector strategy

Firstly, you'll need to decide how you want to approach your data project; you can either take a business-led or data-led approach:

1. Business-led approach

A business-led approach starts with the business requirements:

- ✓ you select all the data sources that seem relevant;
- ✓ you incorporate all data fields within these data sources; and
- ✓ you end up with a large dataset.

The risk with this approach is that you may include more data than you need, increasing your data storage and data processing time. Nevertheless, it's more likely that you'll deliver results quickly with this approach.

2. Data-led approach

A data-led approach starts with the specific data fields that are required in the final output:

✓ you only include the specific data fields; and

✓ you therefore have a focused dataset.

The risk with this approach is that the narrow scope will restrict the flexibility to add more data fields in future. However, it's more likely that you'll end up with a lean, speedy result.

Which one is the best data connector strategy for your business? It will depend on your data project and your business requirements. If you want the quickest solution, go for the business-led approach. If you want the leanest dataset you can get, go for the data-led approach.

Secondly, you'll need to map the business logic to the data fields so that you'll represent the right data in the final output. Not all data fields are labelled in an obvious way that matches the business logic, so this can often take some time to do, and it requires the input of both the data-source manager and the business user.

For instance:

BUSINESS REQUIREMENT	DATA SOURCE	TABLE	DATA FIELD
Monthly Revenue	SAGE – financial tool	Revenue	month_revenue_actual
Customer Volume	HubSpot – CRM tool	Organisations	count_client_organisation
Email Response Rate	MailChimp – email tool	Metrics	clickthrough_rate

Depending on the size of your project and the volume of data fields, this could take hours or days of work, but it's well worth the investment of time to guarantee that you'll extract the data fields you need and you'll interpret them correctly. It's also worthwhile checking your logic with the manager of each data source to confirm your understanding is correct. In my experience, many data field names are not self-explanatory!

Do you need a template or some help with this? Check out the Data Escalator Resources chapter at the end of the book.

Finding the unique identifier(s)

Next, you need to determine what your unique identifiers are; these are data fields that have a unique number or code for each asset, whether they represent a unique customer, employee, partner, project, part or other business asset.

Usually, a business will have unique identifiers such as the following:

- Customer reference number
- Employee ID
- Customer order number
- Invoice number
- Transaction number
- Customer service number
- Part number

These unique identifiers must do what the name suggests: they must be distinct for each asset that they represent. There can be no duplicates. Hence, there needs to be a robust process for which there is a single source of unique identifiers issued in your business. If you don't have any, set them up, as you'll need them to match and combine data sources together to generate advanced insight from your data. Using a unique identifier is by far the best way to do this.

Combining the data

Where there is a unique identifier available, data can be combined and matched across data sources. Where the unique identifier is missing, business logic can be applied instead, including the following:

Manual matching process

For instance:

* It's possible to match business names, but they could be spelt differently, so there might need to be a combination of matching rules covering the business name and the business postcode

* It's possible to match customer names, but, again, they could be spelt differently, so there might need to be a combination of matching rules covering the customer's surname and their date of birth

Fuzzy matching process

For instance:

* When matching names, you can set up fuzzy (or estimated) logic to allow different spellings to be permitted (eg John, Johnathon, Jonathan or J)

* When matching postcodes, you can set up fuzzy logic to allow different lengths of postcode to be permitted (eg BS1 XYZ, BS1 or BS)

Master data sources

For instance:

* If there is a difference in data between the different data sources, business logic should be enforced to always expect one data source to be assumed to be more accurate than the other(s); this can be defined as the primary vs secondary or master vs slave data source

For some projects, this can be a quick process and can be delivered in hours. For a large business, with multiple data sources and legacy systems, this can take days or weeks to accomplish. Sometimes, a manual process is required, particularly if the volumes are low and the matching rules are hard to define.

Extracting, transforming and loading the data

The next step is to extract data from each of the required data sources, transform it into processed output and load it into a new database. This will enable you to analyse the combined dataset. This is ETL – extract, transform and load.

There are several things to consider at this stage:

a. **Timeliness** – Does the data need to be live and updated in real time for the purpose of your data project? Or is daily, weekly or monthly updates sufficient?

b. **Consistency** – Will the data be consistent for the life of your data project? Or will some data sources or data fields change?

c. **Security** – Is the data source within your control and with no security access procedures, such as internal data? Or are you connecting to a third-party data source where authentication is required?

d. **Formatting** – What formats are you going to use for dates, times, locations and similar categorisations?

e. **History** – Do you need to be able to show time-stamped data and changes in data over time?

The answers to these questions will impact how much and how frequently data is extracted and stored. This will influence the speed and cost of your data project, both for the set-up and the ongoing costs. So, it's important to challenge the answers to these questions and not just do what the business has always done. You could save your business tens, hundreds or thousands of pounds per month.

Data connection tools

Should you use a third-party data tool or should you do it all in-house using your own programming code? There's no easy answer to that question, as there are a number of considerations:

- **Budget** – You'll need to consider the development, and set-up and ongoing licence costs for the tool against the manual cost, time and effort of your team programming/coding it themselves.

- **Tool preferences** – Some businesses prefer Microsoft tools, some prefer Amazon and some prefer Google; aligning the tools with the pre-existing platforms used within your business already might fast-track approval by stakeholders. But you should always critically evaluate what's been used in the past, as there could be substantial cost savings to be realised.

- **In-house capability** – You'll need to consider the skills, experience and knowledge within your team to assess their capability to do their own coding, use open-source code or use a licensed software tool.

- **Team preferences** – Depending on your development team, you'll often find that software engineers prefer hand-crafting their own code so that solutions can be tailored, whereas BI engineers prefer off-the-shelf tools so that they can get to the insight more quickly. Again, you should always critically evaluate what's been done in the past, as there could be significant benefits to implementing alternative solutions.

- **Best-in-class** – Some businesses want the latest big thing. Snowflake and Looker are making the technology headlines today, for instance, so consider what's hot right now in your selection process. But you need to ensure that they meet your specific business requirements and that they're not just a fad.

Here are some pros and cons of using a third-party tool vs doing your own programming/coding in-house:

USING A THIRD-PARTY TOOL	PROGRAMMING/CODING IN-HOUSE
Pros	
Easier to set up	No licence fees
Easier to support	Ability to create a tailored, bespoke solution
The tool provider can support you before, during and after your data project	Proprietary solution that could create new intellectual property (IP) for your business
Regular service upgrades are included	
Cons	
Licence fees for as long as you use the tool	Takes longer to set up
Licence fees for all users	The code will need ongoing support by one or more experienced developers
Higher licence fees the more you use the tool	
Examples	
Tools include Matillion, Fivetran, Singer and Pentaho	Python is a popular object-orientated programming language
Cloud-linked tools include Azure Data Factory, Amazon Web Services (AWS) Glue and Google Cloud Platform (GCP) Data Flow	Spark, C# and JavaScript are also used, depending on the requirements for the data project and the developers' experience
Serverless tools are those for which you do not have to maintain a server in-house, so your data solution is distributed across many servers and is therefore scalable; these tools include Snowflake, AWS S3, AWS Aurora, AWS DynamoDB and GCP Firestore	Open source (free to use, modify and redistribute) tools include Apache Kafka, Apache Airflow and Talend's Stitch, which is partially open source
Other vendors include RedBricks and Talend for a wider choice on independent tooling	

Tools and technology are evolving all the time, so do your research before you select one for your business. We use different combinations of these tools, depending on the requirements for each project.

Connecting your data

Can you see how all your data sources connect to each other? You should. You'll need to know how your data sources connect together or if they don't. Hence, the next step is to create a data map showing the data connections and the unique identifiers used.

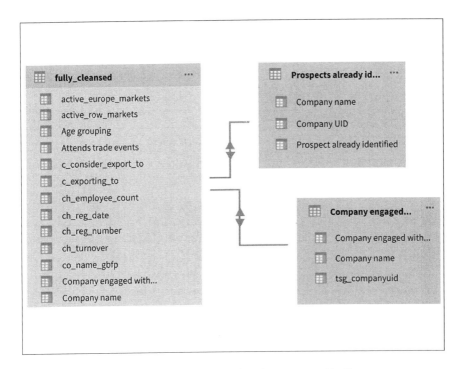

Figure 2: Example of data mapping and matching using unique identifiers

This will allow you to see all your data sources in one place, and to understand if/how they're connected to other data sources or if they work in isolation.

You now know how to connect all your data sources together, so you can do interesting things with your data. You can unite multiple data sources that are disconnected and disparate. You can analyse different data sources together in combination, which gives a greater potential for more valuable insight generation. Can you see how this will help you to generate cross-departmental business insight?

Now you know where the dots are, *you can join them up.*

REAL-WORLD EXAMPLE #4
AN ENERGY BUSINESS

Now I'm going to share a data-connection-related case study with you to turn the principles explained in this step into a real-life example to make this more interesting. Connecting data can be tricky, so here's how we approached it for an energy business.

THE BUSINESS

An energy business

THE DATA PROBLEM

This is a high-growth UK business working in a highly competitive and commoditised market. With a UK headquarters-focused structure and one core service offering, this business is technology led. The business is built around key account activity and strong customer service. Its data covers energy collection, storage and usage, and is sourced from multiple sites. With high-frequency transactions on a cloud IT architecture, there are energy-monitoring reports every minute. Big data is the challenge for this business.

THE DATA OPPORTUNITY

- To automate internal business processes to save manual work

- To automate business reporting for clients to save manual work

- To reduce the risk of errors

THE DATA PROCESS

1. Business requirements – A workshop was run with the key business stakeholders to understand their business requirements for report automation.

2. Process review – The business processes and business logic were reviewed to understand what business activities could be automated.

3. Data-connector strategy – A business-led data approach was selected, as the massive volumes of data meant that only a fraction of the data available was required to meet the business need.

4. Unique identifiers – These were determined for all assets, so a comprehensive assessment of the data hierarchy and data matching was conducted to help with automation.

5. Data ETL – The big data challenge needed to be tackled. Data was being collected at a frequency of minutes from multiple sources, so the volume of data was massive and required high levels of data processing time and data storage.

6. Tools – A bespoke Python data-processing approach was selected due to the specific requirements for the data solution.

7. Data connectivity – Data was connected from multiple sources and at high frequencies, ready to be automated into user-facing reports.

THE RESULT

The data connection work meant that fully automated internal and client-facing reporting could be created. This saved the business time, reduced the need for manual intervention significantly and improved the quality of the user-facing outputs.

THE STEP #4 DATA CONNECTION TIP

For this company, the business logic was highly detailed and complex. There was a need to invest significant time up front to be able to understand the detailed business requirements, so that the data could be mapped, extracted, connected, formatted and analysed in the right way. Without this investment of effort up front, the data wouldn't have been connected in the right way for this specific business need.

LESSONS LEARNT #4
CONNECT YOUR DATA

I also have a wealth of real-world experience with helping various businesses to join their disparate, disconnected data sources. Therefore, so as to prevent you from making those exact same errors in your business on Step #4 of the Data Escalator, here are some of those I've encountered frequently and what I've learnt from them.

1. MOST DATA PROJECTS DON'T NEED REAL-TIME DATA

There's a point in every project when a stakeholder says they want data in real time. Around 99% of the time (that's a made-up statistic), they don't need real-time data. Depending on your project and the business levers you can pull using the data insight, daily data refreshes are often good enough. If you genuinely need to make decisions in real time, such as resource decisions in a call centre, then you'll need real-time data. But if your business will make decisions to pull business levers on a daily, weekly or monthly basis, then having a daily data view is probably right for your business. This will save a lot of money when it comes to data processing, data transfer and storage costs.

2. START WITH WHAT YOU'VE GOT

If you're a Microsoft house, start there. If you're already using Azure, start there. Ditto for Google, Python, etc. If you've already got some components in place, review how they're working for your business first, before considering any brand-new platforms. Starting with what you've got in place at present will save you time, money and effort, and it'll also be easier to convince your stakeholders that you're evolving and improving the business's current capability, rather than starting from scratch.

3. BENEFIT FROM THIRD-PARTY TOOLS

Whilst you can write code to connect your data, there are plenty of off-the-shelf tools you can use that will make your job easier to set up, easier to manage and easier to evolve. Some of them are open source, so are free to use, modify and redistribute. Many of them are low cost and well within most businesses' budgets. They often come with free training provided, so your team can become confident tool users. But be careful of vendor lock-in – you must understand what happens if you want to stop using the tool in future.

4. SPEND MORE ON SET-UP THAN RUNNING COSTS

It's well worth investing up front, to ensure that your ongoing running costs are as low as they can be. The right data architecture will save you thousands or even tens of thousands of pounds every year in future. A smart, upfront design will quickly pay for itself over time. Always create a short-term and long-term budget for your data-tool options; the ones that cost the most in year one might be the lowest cost over the mid to long term.

5. BE RUTHLESS IN THE PURSUIT OF VALUABLE DATA

At this stage of the project, valuable data can fall out of a project just because it's tricky to combine with other data sources. If the data could enable you to generate valuable insight, work hard to get the data included. Use fuzzy matching and use business logic. So long as you can explain the assumptions and the resulting risks, then working hard to keep data within your project is the right thing to do at this stage. But if the data isn't vital, ditch it.

You'll also learn your own lessons as your data connection experience evolves, and you'll improve continually and grow in confidence as you do.

TASK #4 – CREATE YOUR DATA MAP

Before you continue, your next task is to create a data map.

Take 10–20 minutes to start this now.

Show all data sources to be included in this project:

Show any connections between these data sources, and highlight any unique identifiers.

You can develop this further in the coming days, weeks and months of your data project.

Do you need a template or some help with this? Check out the Data Escalator Resources chapter at the end of the book.

STEP #5

PROCESS YOUR DATA

*If you don't know the risks,
you can't mitigate them*

STEP #5 – PROCESS YOUR DATA

When it comes to data processing, it's all about storing your data robustly, securely and logically. Working with data can be high risk, particularly when you're working with confidential, commercially sensitive data or personally identifiable information (PII).

We've all seen news reports on data hacks, thefts and loss; these events result in press coverage, reputational damage, customer loss and fines. So, data and information security should be at the core of any data project. Data must be stored, processed and transferred securely. Risks should be identified, explored and mitigated up front as well as reviewed regularly. Your data strategy and business strategy depend on it.

Running a data health check

Now you've got a data catalogue, a data dictionary and a data map, you need to understand how good your data is. So, let's check the health of all of your data sources and data fields. You can use a five-point process covering the following:

1. **Completeness**

   - Is there any missing data?
   - For each data field, what percentage of the records have that field populated?
   - For each data field, what percentage of the records contain a null value in that field?

2. Uniqueness

- Are there any duplicate records based on the unique identifiers?
- For each data field, what percentage of the records have duplicates in that field?
- For each data field, what percentage of the records have a unique value for that field?

3. Consistency

- Is all the data in a consistent format (eg date, time and location)?
- For each data field, what percentage of the records have a consistent format for that field?
- For each data field, what percentage of the records do not have that field in a consistent format?

4. Timeliness

- Is the data up to date (eg are there records with the latest timestamp)?
- For each data source and data field, what is the date and time of the most recent data input or edit?

5. Accuracy

- Is the data accurate?
- Does it sound right to your stakeholders?
- For each data field, do the volume and/or total value match your stakeholder's expectations?

Depending on the size of your data, you can either do this using a simple tool, such as Excel, or you can ask a programmer to write some code to analyse the data for you.

Do you need a template or some help with this? Check out the Data
Escalator Resources chapter at the end of the book.

By running this process for all your data sources, you'll have a clear idea of
the following:

- What data is good enough to be used for data analysis

- What data is incomplete and needs more work to fill the gaps

- What data is inconsistent and needs more work to process, cleanse or
sort it into a useful format

This process is also a great way to play back your understanding of the
data to your stakeholders. You might find that they realise that they have
forgotten to tell you that a data source has been switched off and replaced
with a new tool, for instance. Or that there's another data source they'd
forgotten to mention to you. The health check is a great way to realise these
types of mistakes and omissions early.

Filling the data gaps

At this stage, most data projects will identify gaps in the data. This is normal,
and there are several options available to you when you identify these data
gaps (see table on the next page).

The right option will depend on the following:

- How important the data field is to your business and this project

- How many gaps you have

- If an alternative data source exists

- How much effort it would take to fill the gaps manually

- How much effort it would take to automate the gap-filling process

UNIMPORTANT DATA GAPS	IMPORTANT DATA GAPS
EXAMPLE #1	EXAMPLE #1
If you're missing the gender identifier for 70% of your customers, but you don't need it for your data project	If you're missing the gender identifier for 70% of your customers, but it's important for your data project
ACTION None	OPTIONS 1. Ask each customer to complete the gender data field retrospectively, but that might take too long 2. Complete the field manually, but that might require too much effort 3. Guesstimate the gender, based on first names, and accept the risk of incorrect gender allocation
EXAMPLE #2	EXAMPLE #2
If you're missing the business-sector identifier for 90% of your business customers, but you don't need it for your data project	If you're missing the business-sector identifier for 90% of your customers, but it's important for your data project
ACTION None	OPTIONS 1. Ask each customer to complete the sector data field retrospectively, but that might take too long 2. Complete the field manually by looking up the company and adding the right sector, but that might require too much effort 3. Use a direct data link from Companies House or similar, where available

UNIMPORTANT DATA GAPS	IMPORTANT DATA GAPS
EXAMPLE #3	EXAMPLE #3
If you're missing the date-of-birth field for 30% of your customers, but you don't need it for your data project	If you're missing the date-of-birth field for 30% of your customers, and it's important for your data project
ACTION None	OPTIONS 1. Ask each customer to complete the date-of-birth field retrospectively, but that might take too long 2. Estimate their year of birth using their age (if available) and use age groups instead

Hence, you'll need to select the right solution for your business and for your data project. And sometimes you'll just have to accept that the data isn't available.

Storing data

The right data-storage solution for your business will depend on your business requirements:

a. **Structured** – Does the data need to be structured, consistent and accessible to many users? If so, choose a database such as SQL.

b. **Operational** – Does the data need to serve an operational-transaction requirement and is it likely to be changeable? If so, choose a NoSQL database such as MongoDB, AWS DynamoDB, GCP Firestore or Azure NoSQL; or select a structured serverless solution such as AWS Aurora, Azure Cosmos DB or GCP Cloud Datastore. MySQL is popular in this area due to being open source and very accessible.

c. **Volume** – Do you have large volumes of data with high cost implications? If so, choose cloud storage such as AWS S3, Azure Blob or GCP Storage. But remember to create your data catalogue, so that you avoid creating a data swamp!

d. **Accessibility** – Does the data need to be readily accessible? If not, choose cold or archive storage, such as AWS Glacier. Each of the cloud storage solutions now has the option to change the storage class to fine tune the price vs accessibility ratio.

e. **Size** – Is the data going to be used for small/medium analytical workloads? If so, a database such as MySQL will do the job.

f. **Frequency** – Is the data going to be used for intensive analytical workloads? If so, choose a massive parallel-processing database such as Google BigQuery, AWS Redshift or Azure Synapse; or one of the new breed of distributed data warehouses such as Snowflake and Firebolt.

g. **Analytics** – Is the data simple and required for analytics? If so, choose data virtualisation over storage, such as AWS S3 with AWS Athena, or go back to the MySQL option.

You'll want to restrict access to your data. All the database solutions mentioned so far have the option to use database credentials to restrict access to specified users. Areas to consider here are as follows:

a. **Location** – Do you need to restrict access to the database itself, to when data is in transit, or to both?

b. **Rules** – Are you going to allow access only to specific individuals, or will you have open access to everyone and just restrict access on an exception basis?

c. **Network** – Do you have a virtual private network (VPN) or a single-sign-on method that your business uses already to restrict access to employees? If so, does your data security need to work with this approach too?

    d. Password management – Will you enforce a need for complex password setting, regular password changes, and/or enforce two-factor or multi-factor authentication?

You'll also want to back up your data for business continuity reasons, in the event of data loss. Think about your appetite for data loss and consider:

* Frequency – *How often should data be backed up?*

* Timeliness – *How long should backups be retained for?*

* Extent – *Does all the data need to be backed up or just some of the data?*

The answers to these questions will determine the speed of data storage and processing time, as well as the cost of backups. So, you'll have to balance cost with reduced risk through regular backups. Many businesses use a process of daily backups, where backups are stored for 30 days and then deleted permanently, as an example of balancing the need for backups with cost.

You should also consider having different data storage for different needs. Separating out development work from operational production data is good practice.

There are three separate areas to consider:

1. **Development** – This is where developers can work independently of each other to develop new features without impacting any operational systems.

2. **Testing** – This is where developers merge work together and test the system's integration points to upstream or downstream systems, and where business stakeholders can test the system against their original business requirements.

3. **Production** – This is where systems are deployed to for final use by their intended end users.

This topic alone could fill a whole new book, so this is an area to explore in detail with a data expert. Consult an experienced data architect or data engineer, explain your business requirements to them, and they'll recommend the best solution for your business.

> There are many data storage and processing tools on the market;
> I've mentioned some already, but technology changes rapidly,
> so I recommend you check out G2's data warehouse grid
> for the latest assessment of tools on the market:
> https://www.g2.com/categories/data-warehouse#grid.

Keeping you legal

There are rules, regulations and laws that every business owner and data processor must be aware of and plan for. The key one for businesses with UK and European customers or users is the General Data Protection Regulation (GDPR).

Some data is higher risk than other data, so it's worth focusing particularly on these data types:

- ✓ Personally identifiable information (PII) – This is data on individuals, and it includes names, dates of birth, addresses and other unique identifiers.

- ✓ High-value data – This is data that will be attractive to thieves, and it includes credit card details, bank account details, usernames and passwords.

- ✓ Highly confidential data – This is data that many people wouldn't want to be made available to others, and it includes sexuality, gender, race and medical information.

- ✓ Commercially sensitive data – This is data that your business wouldn't want made publicly available, and it includes financial data, customer lists, employee data and any intellectual property within the data.

If you need to extract, analyse or visualise data that fits into any of these categories, your data security risks are significantly higher, and therefore your data security processes need to be significantly more stringent.

GDPR states four main rules that any business needs to be prepared for:

1. **Processing rules** – Data must be processed lawfully. This means that data is processed only in the ways that you have permission to do so, and that the data subjects, such as your customers, are aware that you'll process their data in this way. This rule is to safeguard that you don't use data incorrectly, illegally or unethically. Ask yourself whether you would be happy if your data was processed in this way.

2. **Profiling rules** – Customer data must be profiled in a fair, accurate and transparent way. When creating customer profiles, there is a danger that data could be misinterpreted and simplified. This rule is to ensure that profiling rules are legal and transparent. Ask yourself whether your profiling work could be discriminatory.

3. **Data-subject rules** – Data subjects (eg customers) must be able to access their data, ask for it to be deleted and ask to transfer it. This rule reminds you that the data on your customers or users does not belong to your business: it belongs to your customer or user. So, if they want to access the data you hold on them, you need to make it available to them. Ask yourself whether you can do this.

4. **Notification rules** – A data breach must be reported to the authorities quickly and accurately. This rule should be the most obvious of all the rules. If data is hacked, if data is lost or if data is stolen, you need to report it. Ask yourself whether you know whom to tell, and when and what to tell them.

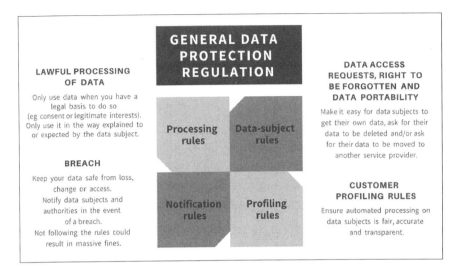

Figure 3: GDPR overview of the data processing rules

I highly recommend that every business undertakes a data protection impact assessment to make certain that you fully understand the risks for your business. This can be self-assessed using a simple-to-use process from the Information Commissioners Office (ICO): https://ico.org.uk/for-organisations/data-protection-self-assessment/.

For any data project, you need to have a decent understanding of the regulations relating to data, as well as a working knowledge of GDPR. This is an area to seek external help if you don't have the expertise within your business already.

Good vs bad data usage

We all know what 'bad' looks like when it comes to data: data breaches, selling data to third parties without permission, GDPR fines and customer complaints, to name a few. But what does 'good' data usage look like? Where is the line between bad and good?

Some of the things I often get asked by businesses are 'May we do this?', 'Is it allowed?', 'Are we GDPR compliant?' and 'Are we risking a fine?' It's rarely a simple answer, as – although we know what bad looks like, it's trickier to be confident in what good looks like.

Businesses use data in a good way when it's useful, permitted and expected. For instance, when a business makes it easier for you to do business with it or gives you loyalty points or discounts, like a supermarket chain does. We can categorise good data usage as being secure, compliant and useful.

However, businesses can go too far and turn from good to not so good. For instance, when a business sends too many or irrelevant emails to you or contacts you too much through any channel. We can categorise not-so-good data usage as being irrelevant, intrusive and unhelpful.

And, of course, there are the catastrophically bad data usage examples. For instance, selling data without permission, losing data or getting hacked. These are the examples that make you close your account and go elsewhere, after updating all your passwords in a panic. We can categorise bad data usage as being risky, irresponsible and unexpected.

In reality, it's not this simple. Many businesses have complex business processes, multiple decision-makers, and bespoke products and services. Therefore, the line isn't as easy to see as in the examples listed so far. So, how can we define good vs bad data usage? (See the diagram on the following page for examples of good vs bad data usage.)

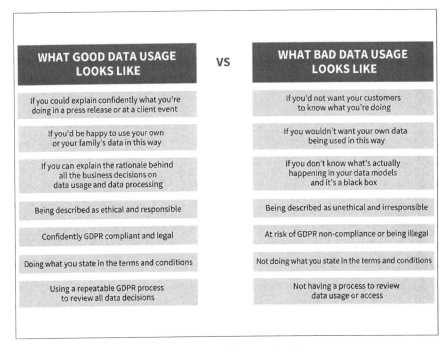

WHAT GOOD DATA USAGE LOOKS LIKE	VS	WHAT BAD DATA USAGE LOOKS LIKE
If you could explain confidently what you're doing in a press release or at a client event		If you'd not want your customers to know what you're doing
If you'd be happy to use your own or your family's data in this way		If you wouldn't want your own data being used in this way
If you can explain the rationale behind all the business decisions on data usage and data processing		If you don't know what's actually happening in your data models and it's a black box
Being described as ethical and responsible		Being described as unethical and irresponsible
Confidently GDPR compliant and legal		At risk of GDPR non-compliance or being illegal
Doing what you state in the terms and conditions		Not doing what you state in the terms and conditions
Using a repeatable GDPR process to review all data decisions		Not having a process to review data usage or access

Figure 4: Comparison of good data usage vs bad data usage

The more anonymised and aggregated the data, the more confident you can be. However, you need to be incredibly careful when dealing with PII and, particularly, with sensitive data, such as medical information or categorisations that could potentially be used to be discriminatory. In addition, using data internally is lower risk than when you share data outside of your business. Let's map it out in terms of risk levels:

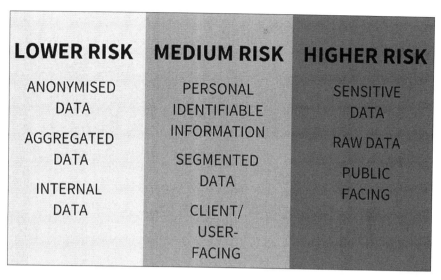

Figure 5: Risk levels by data type

This can be subjective, and therefore prone to different interpretations by different people. If in doubt, seek external help.

Mitigating data risks

I've talked a lot about risk and regulations in this step of the Data Escalator. Hence, you might be feeling anxious right now. The best way to deal with risk is head on. I recommend you analyse your data risks using a standard risk-assessment approach:

#	RISK NAME	DESCRIPTION	PROBABILITY OF OCCURRING	IMPACT IF RISK OCCURS	MITIGATING ACTION
1	Theft/Hack	Unauthorised internal/external data access	LOW	HIGH	Cybersecurity consultation
2	Deletion	Staff member deletes data field / source	MEDIUM	MEDIUM	Restrict access rights
3	Costs	Storage costs are higher than expected	HIGH	LOW	Monitor monthly

This process will allow you to get input from people working with you across your business, which will encourage them to share any risks that they can see. It's a great method to encourage your team, your users and your stakeholders to talk openly with you about their concerns and worries, rather than keeping them to themselves.

Using this process will also reassure you and your stakeholders that you have considered all risks carefully and planned mitigating actions.

Wherever possible, anonymise your data. This will significantly reduce your risk. For instance, remove the names of customers if you're looking at aggregated customer trends. Use age groups rather than dates of birth when you're looking at customer-segment analysis. Use the first three digits of a postcode, rather than the address and full postcode when you're looking at aggregated regional trends. Put simply, don't extract any data that you won't use in your data project.

You now know how to store, process and transfer your data robustly, securely and logically. You can be confident working with commercially sensitive data or PII, because data and information security will be at the core of your data project. You can share risks with your team and stakeholders, and then implement mitigating actions. You can reduce risk through anonymisation and aggregation. Can you see how this will significantly improve your chances of success with your data project?

Now you know the risks, *you can mitigate them.*

REAL-WORLD EXAMPLE #5
A UK FINANCIAL SERVICES SME

This actual example is a data processing related case study, which puts the theory described in this step into a practical, tactical context. The experience of a UK financial services SME reveals some of the usual challenges you might face in this area.

THE BUSINESS

A UK financial services SME

THE DATA PROBLEM

This is a high-growth, scale-up UK business. It has a UK headquarters with multiple business departments. With multiple service offerings and multiple products, this business has a critical supplier and distribution network. Service-wide key account, client and supplier activities are core to the customer service ethos. Its data covers business customers, product sales, service usage and financials, which are stored in multiple places. With a cloud IT architecture, and a range of third-party platforms and tools, the data is disconnected and siloed.

THE DATA OPPORTUNITY

- To automate internal business processes to reduce manual work

- To automate business reporting for clients to reduce manual work

- To automate supplier reporting to reduce manual work

THE DATA PROCESS

1. Business requirements – A series of workshops were run to capture business requirements across the business.

2. Data health check – The data was analysed using the five-point data health check, focusing particularly on data completeness and uniqueness.

3. Data gaps – Gaps were identified between the business requirements and the data availability, where data was either missing, incomplete or hadn't been captured.

4. Data storage – As the business already used cloud data storage, the data project continued to use this solution alongside data tools, including Snowflake and Matillion.

5. Data regulation – A comprehensive GDPR review and due-diligence process were undertaken to safeguard that all data work would comply with UK law and with the business's terms and conditions for its customers.

6. Data risks – Risks were identified, discussed, logged and mitigated. The main risk focused on restricting data access to only the people who needed access to the data, through a permissions-based approach.

THE RESULT

Comprehensive data-processing work enabled the creation of fully automated internal and client-facing reporting, which saved the business time, significantly reduced the need for manual intervention and improved the quality of data outputs. This resulted in more money being invested into data, in the form of people and budgets for future data projects.

THE STEP #5 DATA PROCESSING TIP

For this business, the key element was building on the existing capability and integrating with existing business processes. This meant that the key stakeholders felt confident that the data processing work was an evolution of what had been done before, and this was reassuring when it came to performing risk assessments and regulatory assessments.

LESSONS LEARNT #5
PROCESS YOUR DATA

Through assisting many businesses to process their data in a secure, robust and scalable way, I have gained much experience. There are many common mistakes that I've run into and lessons I've learnt, which I'll share with you to help safeguard your business against repeating the same errors in your business on Step #5 of the Data Escalator.

1. DON'T LET GDPR SCARE YOU

I know businesses that have been so scared of receiving a GDPR fine that they have deleted data. That's not necessary. You need to treat data with due care and attention, of course, but you can and should use your data for good too. GDPR aims to protect individuals' data. But you can do this and still use data to provide an enhanced, improved customer service. So don't be scared, be sensible.

2. ANONYMISE DATA WHEREVER YOU CAN

To reduce your risk when it comes to data, anonymise data wherever and whenever you can. You can aggregate data for trend analysis. You can use only the data you need for a project, not all data available. You can remove PII. You can make sure you don't include any commercially sensitive or highly personal data in your data project at all. If you don't need it, don't use it. Simple.

3. PUT DATA SECURITY AT THE HEART OF THE SOLUTION

No one wants a data hack, theft or loss. So you should plan for the worst to happen, right from the outset. Construct your data solution with data security built in to every level. Unless your data project uses publicly available data, you'll want to restrict access to your data to specific users. Build in controls, test your controls, document your controls and review them regularly.

4. DATA GAPS CAN BE FILLED

Most, if not all, data projects find data gaps. But they can be filled in a multitude of ways, so if the missing data is required, fill the gaps. The sooner you do it, the sooner you can benefit from having that data. Plus, the data gaps usually get bigger as you grow. Hence, the sooner you fill them, the better. Don't ignore data gaps; make a plan to fill them, even if it takes time to do so.

5. SELECT THE RIGHT TOOL FOR YOUR BUSINESS NEED

If you're a small SME, you need to select a tool for SMEs, not one for large enterprises, and vice versa. Don't just use what you've used in other businesses, as it may not be fit for purpose in your current business. Not all business needs are the same. Not all business data is the same. Not all data projects are the same. So, there's no one-size-fits-all data tool for every business need. Don't just jump on the latest tool bandwagon. Focus on your specific data needs and select the right tool for the job.

You'll also learn your own lessons as your data processing experience evolves, and you'll improve continually and grow in confidence as you do.

TASK #5 – CREATE YOUR DATA PROCESSING PLAN

Before you continue, let's create a data processing plan.

Take 10–20 minutes to start this now.

TASK	CURRENT STATUS	ACTION
Data Health Check	eg not started, ongoing or complete	eg [owner] to undertake by [date]
Data Protection Impact Assessment	eg not started, ongoing or complete	eg [owner] to undertake by [date]
Data Tool Review	eg not started, ongoing or complete	eg [owner] to undertake by [date]

You can develop this further in the coming days, weeks and months of your data project.

Do you need a template or some help with this? Check out the Data Escalator Resources chapter at the end of the book.

STEP #6

ANALYSE YOUR DATA

If you don't try, you'll never know

STEP #6 – ANALYSE YOUR DATA

When it comes to analysing your data, it can be tricky to know where to start. There are so many ways to analyse data, and so many tools, methodologies, models and statistics available to you. It can feel overwhelming, and there is a risk that you'll get bogged down with analysing every little thing. So, go back to the business needs identified in Step #1 of the Data Escalator and only run the analytics you need to answer your specific business need. Focus on the questions that need to be answered, the hypotheses you're trying to test and the trends you're trying to discover.

Having said that, it's only when you start analysing the data that you'll start to discover new patterns and trends. Hence, whilst you should have a data-analytics plan and a methodology in mind, you also need to keep an open mind to see where the data takes you. You could discover insight that you never knew existed. Therefore, always allow time to play with the data.

Types of analytics

There is a range of different analytical tools at your disposal, and each tool is appropriate for different objectives:

A. Descriptive

This is presenting the key facts shown in the data, such as the following:

- ✓ Headline facts
- ✓ Trends over time
- ✓ Split by region/department/product

This is useful when you want to present a picture of the current state of your business. It is helpful to test the numbers and to check the data is being interpreted correctly. It's a useful first step on any data project and a good way to build stakeholders' trust in the data.

B. Comparative

This is comparing one set of data with another, such as the following:

- ✓ Comparisons by year
- ✓ Comparisons by region, department and/or product
- ✓ Comparisons to the average of the group

This is useful when you want to identify high and low performance across your business. It's a good way to determine high-performing areas to highlight best practice. Plus, it's a good way to isolate problem areas that need attention.

C. Ranking

This is the process to show a prioritised list, such as the following:

- ✓ Best-performing products
- ✓ Highest-performing salesperson
- ✓ Worst-performing region

This is useful when you want to reveal high and low performance across your business. It's a good way to target your activity to the highest- or lowest-performing areas first.

D. Personalisation

This is showing data for a defined individual or business, such as the following:

- ✓ A client dashboard showing their data for the last 12 months

✓ An employee scorecard showing their performance vs their targets

✓ A sales dashboard showing the performance of their portfolio

This is useful for providing individual, personalised data to users. It's a good way to add more value to clients or users, and it's a good way for individuals to track their own performance.

E. Predictive

This is using past data and/or external data to forecast business data, such as the following:

✓ Making sales forecasts based on run rate vs current sales targets

✓ Forecasting when customers will exit, so you can retain them

✓ Understanding the impact of external factors on business performance

This is useful to enable a business to mitigate future risks by acting in advance. It's a good way to inform business plans and risk-mitigation plans, and to spot problems and opportunities, then act in advance.

F. Discovery

This is using data to find unknown patterns and trends, such as the following:

✓ Using AI to process big data

✓ Identifying complex and multivariate patterns and trends

✓ Identifying unknown connections and dependencies between data sources

This is useful to enable a business to run advanced algorithms. It gives you the potential to uncover brand-new insights and trends, and to create a competitive advantage.

For most data projects, you'll use a combination of some or all of these types of data analytics. Each type of data-analytics approach will give you a different insight into the data. Some might lead to perceptive discoveries and tell your business something new. Some might lead to nothing. Data analytics is like an experiment, and you never know what you'll discover until you start analysing the data.

Data analytics tools

There are many data analytics tools available for businesses, including these:

ANALYTICS LEVEL	DESCRIPTION	TOOLS
Simple	If your data is small and all in one place, and your analytics needs are descriptive, comparative and ranking	Excel • Low cost • Widely used • Great introductory data analysis tool
Intermediate	If your data is larger, more complex and from multiple sources, and your analytics needs are for personalisation and predictions	Power BI • Part of the Microsoft suite • Easy to use and requires no coding • Good analytics and visualisation tool Tableau • Easy to use and requires no coding • Good analytics and visualisation tool Google Data Studio • Easy to use and requires no coding • Good website analytics tool

ANALYTICS LEVEL	DESCRIPTION	TOOLS
Advanced	If your data is big data, and your analytics needs are for advanced predictions and discovery	R • Programming language • Requires coding expertise Python • Programming language • Requires coding expertise Tensor Flow • AI and ML tools

Whatever tool you use, don't lose sight of the end goal: to deliver actionable insight to your user. It's easy to get engrossed in what tools can do and lose track at this stage. Focus on what the user of the data analytics tool needs.

Statistical tools

How do you know when a pattern or trend is significant? That's where statistical tools come in. These statistical methodologies are great ways to understand, test and size the pattern or trend that you're seeing in the data. You can choose from a variety of statistical calculations, including these:

Mean

This is an average of a set of numbers, achieved by dividing the total sum of the quantities by the number of them. The mean is useful for when you want to give an overview of a dataset. It is quick and easy to calculate, but it may hide the impact of extreme high/low values that might skew the data.

Standard deviation

This measures the spread of values around the mean value. Standard deviation is useful for showing you the range of data within a dataset:

- A high value shows a high difference between the mean value and other data values, so a high data dispersion
- A low value shows a small difference between the mean value and other data values, so a low data dispersion

But, again, the value may be skewed by extreme values.

Regression

This is useful for revealing the relationship between two datasets. A regression line is given on a scatter plot, showing data for one variable against another, but correlation does not mean causation, so trends need to be treated as hypotheses, not as cause and effect.

Spearman's rank correlation coefficient

This shows the strength and direction of a relationship between datasets. Spearman's rank is useful for illustrating the relationship between two datasets:

- The result will always be between +1 and -1
- A value of +1 indicates a perfect positive relationship
- A value of zero indicates no relationship
- A value of -1 indicates a perfect negative relationship
- The closer it is to zero, the weaker the relationship

Chi squared

This shows how likely it is that an observed relationship between datasets is due to chance. Chi squared is useful for testing a hypothesis. It's called a 'goodness of fit' measure because it illustrates how well the observed data fits with the expected data.

The methodologies behind these statistical tools are easy to find using a Google search or in a statistics textbook.

Statistics are a great way to test, size and validate the patterns and trends you discover. You can use statistics to explain the significance of your data insight to your users, so your insight is objective. Statistics can also be used to explain the risk that patterns and trends may be insignificant, so it's a useful way to make sure your users understand how to interpret the results. For instance, a correlation for which there is high confidence should be considered more seriously than a correlation for which there is low confidence. However, just remember, don't dazzle your data users with statistics, but ensure that everything you share with them is clear, simple and easy to explain.

Unstructured data analytics

In Step #3 of the Data Escalator, we discussed unstructured data, which could include text, audio, video, imagery, commentary and/or descriptions. When it comes to data analysis for unstructured data, you have two options:

1. **Convert the unstructured data into structured data so it's easier to analyse**

2. **Leave it unstructured**

To convert unstructured data into structured data, you can use a variety of options:

a. **Words, sentences, descriptions and commentary**

You can convert unstructured data of this type into structured data in one of these ways:

- Extract the frequently used words or phrases
- Count the number of times a word or phrase has been used
- Calculate the positive and negative sentiment by analysing words defined as positive or negative (being careful of the use of sarcasm!)

For instance, this could work well for survey feedback, social media comments and call centre recordings.

b. Imagery and video

You can convert unstructured data of this type into structured data as follows:

- ○ Extract key information, such as the volume, frequency, size and/or speed of a defined object
- ○ Extract information on the date and time, or size, format and/or labels of the data

For instance, this could work well for satellite imagery and video camera footage.

In both cases, you must remember that you're simplifying and summarising the data. You're losing data richness, and therefore potentially missing the opportunity to discover deeper insight.

If you think it could be valuable to leave the data unstructured, you'll need to use AI and ML methodologies to analyse it instead, as outlined in the next section.

Artificial intelligence (AI) and machine learning (ML)

There's a lot of jargon when it comes to data analysis, so let's bust some of it!

AI

Artificial intelligence – 'The theory and development of computer systems able to perform tasks normally requiring human intelligence, such as visual perception, speech recognition, decision-making, and translation between languages.'[3]

---

3. Artificial intelligence (n.d.). In Lexico.com dictionary. Retrieved from https://www.lexico.com/definition/artificial_intelligence

AI enables us to run more complex and advanced data analyses than we can if we do it manually, and at a far quicker speed.

ML

This is an application of AI that provides systems with the ability to automatically learn and improve from experience, without being explicitly programmed. ML is used to analyse big, unstructured datasets in a rapid time. ML often is guided by or has interference from an individual to set the terms of the analysis, such as classifying data or defining a goal. For example, this could be used for analysing all of the complexities and patterns within a big dataset, and then using these patterns to create forecasting models.

Supervised ML

This is when an individual guides the ML model to focus on specific data inputs or outputs; for instance, if we ask ML to find a pattern between X and Y using specific variables. For example, this could be used for forecasting sales performance for a new client, on which you have no data, based on past sales figures across all of your clients, when all you have to compare them on is their size, sector and turnover.

Unsupervised ML

This is when the ML model is used to discovers patterns with no classification of data inputs, outputs or processes; for instance, if ML is used on a raw dataset. For example, this could be used for finding patterns to understand why service levels drop at certain times, when there are so many influencing variables that it would be impossible to do it manually.

Deep learning (DL)

This is a type of ML, but it works with no guidance or interference at all and runs freely on the data. Think about analysing satellite imagery to find patterns and trends that you didn't even know exist.

Natural language processing (NLP)

This is connecting computers with the natural language used by humans. For example, this is used for predictive autocomplete text tools and voice-command tools such as Alexa.

AI is like a big bag of tricks filled with the initialisms ML, DL and NLP. This bag of tricks is great to use when performing advanced analytics, such as when you're creating predictive models, analysing big data and deciphering unstructured data.

This topic alone could fill a whole new book, so this is an area to explore in detail with a data scientist. Consult an experienced data analyst or data scientist, explain your business requirements to them, and they'll recommend the best solution for your business.

You should select the most appropriate analytical tools depending on your data project and your business needs.

You now know how to analyse data. You know which tools, methodologies, models and statistics are available to you. You can confidently run only the analytics you need to answer your specific business need. You can answer the questions that need to be resolved, test the hypotheses you want and explore the trends you're discovering. Can you see that you could discover insight that no one even knew existed?

Now you know what to try, *you'll find out what you don't know.*

REAL-WORLD EXAMPLE #6
AN INSURANCE START-UP

There are never-ending opportunities for data analytics to be used within a business. Hence, I will share a data analytics case study with you here to turn the theory described in this step into reality. This time it's for an insurance start-up experimenting with data.

THE BUSINESS

An insurance start-up

THE DATA PROBLEM

This is a start-up UK insurance business. Like many start-ups, this business has a small team, and an evolving consultancy and product offering. Obtaining data from multiple sources, this business is a data creator, data processor and data purchaser. Its data covers business customers, insurance products and financials, and is stored in multiple places. In this highly competitive market, this start-up is looking for a niche and to create a competitive advantage using data.

THE DATA OPPORTUNITY

- To create innovative ways to display data

- To create a unique customer offering to stand out from the crowd

- To maximise the small volumes of data available

THE DATA PROCESS

1. Business requirements – A workshop with the team was run to define the business vision, review the market, identify a competitive positioning and create the data plan.

2. Data review – The data was reviewed across all the different data sources and then combined.

3. Data analytics – A range of alternative ways to analyse the data was explored to show new and different patterns and trends, using comparative, prioritisation and predictive analytical methods.

4. Statistics – Regression and correlation coefficients were used to test the relationships between data fields, from which the stronger, more relevant correlations were selected.

5. Prototype – The data analytics methodologies and statistical test results were visualised in Power BI, ready for feedback from the business and external stakeholders.

THE RESULT

Innovative data analysis techniques were applied to the core data, and they were used to design a new data driven product, providing a competitive advantage in the market.

THE STEP #6 DATA ANALYTICS TIP

For this business, the key was experimentation. We tried a range of analytical and statistical techniques to analyse the data. Some worked and some didn't. This iterative, test-and-learn approach to data analytics meant that we created an environment that was ripe for innovation and idea generation. Without this experimentation phase, we wouldn't have created such a unique data analytics solution.

LESSONS LEARNT #6
ANALYSE YOUR DATA

Data analytics is a big subject with many opportunities to get lost down a rabbit hole. This book is based on my own experience of helping many businesses to analyse their data, so I wanted to share some of the usual mistakes I've observed and my lessons learnt to help you ensure that you don't repeat those mistakes in your business on Step #6 of the Data Escalator.

1. START SIMPLE

Don't rush straight into ML and predictive models. Start by running simple descriptive analytics so you can understand the basics first. Starting simply makes certain that you spot any missing data or incorrect data early, so it doesn't get lost and inadvertently skew your advanced data analytics, in which errors will be harder to spot and could lead to assumptions being made on incorrect data.

2. CAUSE IS NOT CAUSATION

Just because a pattern exists doesn't necessarily mean something. It could be random or a coincidence. Always evaluate your findings critically before making business decisions. Ask yourself whether this feels right and whether it makes sense. Be careful not to jump to conclusions too early, which could result in your business making the wrong decision and pulling the wrong business levers.

3. DON'T LET THE JARGON OR CODE SCARE YOU

If you don't understand something, just ask. If someone can't explain something to you simply, they probably don't understand it themselves. Therefore, ask questions, search online, educate yourself and talk to people. If you don't understand the data analysis, you won't be able to explain it to your stakeholders when they ask you. This means it's important that you get the clarity you need – don't be afraid of those data scientists and their acronyms/initialisms!

4. DON'T BAFFLE YOUR STAKEHOLDERS WITH COMPLEXITY

I've seen many a presentation where the clever, knowledgeable, hard-working data expert loses the room because they explain all of the technical detail without talking about what it means for the business. Focus on what your stakeholders want. Explain the purpose of the data project and the business levers they'll be able to pull using the new data insight. Skip all the detail on the methodology, coding, statistical models and AI techniques unless they specifically ask you about it.

5. TEST, TEST and TEST AGAIN

Before sharing the insight from your data-analysis work, double-check it. Run the data analysis again. Use some statistical tests to prove or disprove your hypotheses. Make sure you're certain of the result before you share the data insight and, more importantly, before your business starts acting on it. Otherwise, your business could end up making bad business decisions based on incorrect analysis.

You'll also learn your own lessons as your data analytics work evolves, and you'll improve continually and grow in confidence as you do.

TASK #6 – CREATE YOUR DATA ANALYTICS PLAN

Before you continue, let's create a data analytics plan.

Take 10–20 minutes to start this now.

ANALYSIS PLANNING	ANSWERS
ANALYSIS #1	
What data are you using?	
What do you need to find out?	
What type of analytics is required?	
ANALYSIS #2	
What data are you using?	
What do you need to find out?	
What type of analytics is required?	
ANALYSIS #3	
What data are you using?	
What do you need to find out?	
What type of analytics is required?	
ANALYSIS #4	
What data are you using?	
What do you need to find out?	
What type of analytics is required?	

ANALYSIS PLANNING	ANSWERS
ANALYSIS #5	
What data are you using?	
What do you need to find out?	
What type of analytics is required?	

You can develop this further in the coming days, weeks and months of your data project.

Do you need a template or some help with this? Check out the Data Escalator Resources chapter at the end of the book.

STEP #7

VISUALISE YOUR DATA

If it doesn't tell you something, what's the point?

STEP #7 – VISUALISE YOUR DATA

Now you're ready to visualise your data, so you can share patterns, trends and insight with your business. Be warned, though, this always takes longer than you expect. There are tons of ways you can visualise data; loads of graphs you can use; a myriad of statistical results you can show; and endless ways to use colour, icons and branding to personalise your data visualisation.

Whilst it's really easy to create loads of graphs, it's really hard to make data simple. And it's even harder to derive insights from data and tell a perceptive story to your data tool user. Consequently, you should allow sufficient time for data visualisation rather than rushing it at the end.

User-orientated design

Never design a one-size-fits-all solution when it comes to data visualisation. Otherwise, there is a risk that no one will be happy. Always design a data visualisation for a specific user and their specific user requirements. And – to confirm that you fully understand what your user needs – you'll need to capture their business requirements:

USER QUESTIONS	EXAMPLE ANSWERS
What do they do or what's their job?	Marketing director
What's their core objective or primary goal?	To decide where to allocate resources and budget to achieve sales targets
What do they need to know from the data?	How well the marketing activity is performing, including what's on/off target How it compares to last year

143

USER QUESTIONS	EXAMPLE ANSWERS
What decisions will they make using the data or what actions will they take?	How much to spend on which marketing communication channels; eg advertising, PR and/or blogs What tasks should be prioritised over others, based on which activity generates the most leads
What language, labels and/or terms do they use and understand?	We all use different terms for sales conversion rates, so we need to create one consistent language within this project
Do they want high-level information?	Yes, for reporting to the board
Do they want to explore, interrogate and dive into the data in more detail?	Yes, to identify the root causes of problem areas
When will they want to see the data and how often?	Daily updates are required as a minimum
What format does the data need to be in? How will they access it?	Visual, interactive format; it will mainly be accessed on laptops, but sometimes on mobiles
Is the data confidential? Who will access it?	Yes, the data is for our employees only, but any employee in the marketing team needs to be able to view it
Are there any other critical success factors for the data visualisation?	It needs to show our business logo and use our brand colours

I recommend interviewing users either face to face or on the phone, rather than using a survey. This allows you to understand the 'why' as well as the 'what', so you can really discern what they need. In addition, it allows you to check your understanding with them to minimise any misunderstandings. It's really important to challenge what they tell you and double-check that they haven't missed anything; the best way to do this is by playing back to them, in your words, what they told you, to check you've got a complete brief.

Start with a prototype

I recommend creating data-visualisation mock-ups or draft designs, so you can test them with the user(s), get their feedback and ensure it's right before you start work. This will save you considerable time, as it's far easier to make significant changes at this stage, rather than once the data visualisation has been built. It's well worth the effort up front, rather than jumping into building the data visualisation.

Here's an example of a mock-up or a design:

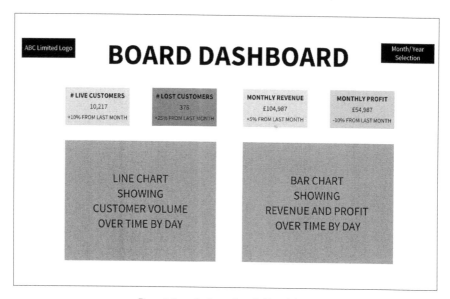

Figure 6: Example of a mock-up dashboard design

It's crucial to check your understanding with your target users at this stage to confirm that your interpretation of their requirements is the same as theirs. I find that this process always highlights a missing requirement or a misunderstood requirement, so it's rarely a waste of time.

Types of visualisations

There are many types of visualisation, such as dashboards, reports, scorecards, report cards, data extracts, BI tools and insights. Are they all the same? Are they totally different? Or somewhere in between?

I will focus on six types of data tool, yet everyone calls them different things, so people can often end up misinterpreting what others mean when referring to dashboards, scorecards and the like.

I work with many people in different roles, in different businesses, in different sectors, of different sizes and with different objectives, but I believe you only need six types of data tool:

1. The scorecard – 'Just show me the key statistics'

This is your all-in-one-place, high-level view. This may be for your board or management team. It will illustrate the core business metrics that they'll want to know about, such as sales, costs and profit numbers. Or you could have an employee scorecard to show personalised performance, such as calls, meetings, sales and conversion rates. The scorecard allows the user to spot high and low performance, so they can take action quickly to investigate the root cause as and when required. It may be used daily, weekly or monthly. Either way, it needs to be simple and do exactly what it needs to – show them the key statistics!

2. The dashboard – 'Give me an overview'

This is your everyday dashboard. Every manager or team in your business should have a dashboard showing how their team, function or department is performing. It allows them to select certain dates, locations or functions, so they can see filtered views if they want to. It will need to be designed specifically for each user, so they can see the data that's important to them. The dashboard allows the user to identify patterns and trends, so they can proceed quickly to implementing improvements or business changes as and when required. It may be used daily, weekly or monthly. Consequently, it needs to be intuitive and meet the user's requirements to give them an overview!

3. The interactive tool – 'Allow me to dive into the data and explore it for myself'

This is a full-on interactive tool. Some people in your business need to be able to dive deep beneath the high-level figures into the data itself. This will facilitate them slicing and dicing the data, or filtering it, in many different ways to see what's really causing a problem. It is essential that this is designed explicitly to meet the requirements of each user, so they can interrogate the data in a way that lets them do their job better. It may be used daily, weekly or monthly. Regardless of timescales, it needs to be thorough, detailed, and let the users dive into the data and explore it for themselves!

4. The data extract – 'Let me export the information I need'

This is your tool for extracting and exporting data. Sometimes, people in your business need to export and extract the data they require into a specific data format, which permits them to create their own analyses or combine it with other data. It will need to be created with the expected user requirements in mind, so that the correct data fields can be extracted in the right format. The data extracts allow the user to get to the data they need, when they need it. It may be used daily, weekly or monthly on demand, or set up as a routine automated task. It needs to be accurate and let the users export the information they need!

5. The insight story – 'Show me what the data tells us, and what we should do about it'

This is your fully developed insight story. Occasionally, you need to forget the numbers and facts, and generate actionable insight. This is a means to identify the 'why' as well as the 'what' behind the data. It will need to be designed to answer a specific question or solve a specific challenge, so you can make smarter, data-driven, insightful decisions. The insight story helps the user to understand what's going on, what's happened in the past and/or what's going to happen in future. It may be used on a one-off-project basis or the insight story may be updated regularly with refreshed data. It needs to be compelling, engaging and give the users insight!

6. The report – 'Tell me everything I need to know'

This provides a professional, slick and stylish report. There are times when you need to pull everything together into a single report. This could be for your senior business leaders, clients, shareholders, employees, market or other stakeholders. It facilitates sharing the results of your business's performance. It must be devised specifically for your target audience, so that they will interpret it in the intended way. The report aids the user in understanding the outcome of any data analysis you've done. Like the insight story, it may be used on a one-off-project basis or the report may be updated regularly with refreshed data. It needs to be thorough, detailed and tell them what they need to know!

In reality, I wouldn't get hung up on the name of the data visualisation output, but it's worth double-checking user requirements before jumping to conclusions about what is meant when referring to a scorecard, dashboard or report.

Selecting the right graph types

When it comes to selecting the right graph, it can feel overwhelming as there are so many to choose from. My advice is to keep it simple; most people don't understand data and feel intimidated by complex graphs. As a result, you should make it easy for them to see the data without dazzling them with unnecessary complexity.

Make it straightforward for them to work out what the data means to them. Don't make them work hard. Keep it simple. (See the table on the next page for some ideas on the types of graphs available and examples of where to use them.)

If you want some inspiration, I love the visual library from the *Financial Times* (https://github.com/ft-interactive/chart-doctor/tree/master/visual-vocabulary), which is well worth exploring.

TYPE	GRAPHS	EXAMPLES
The simple ones	Headline facts	Monthly revenue = £25,795 Customer volume = 213 Customer satisfaction = 87%
	Bar charts	Sales by month Customers by region Profit for 2020 vs 2019
	Line charts	Website visitors over time Sales by country over time Email response rates over time
	Pie charts	Sales percentage by product type Customer volume percentage by region Customer satisfaction percentage by high/ medium/low
The more advanced ones	Scatter plots	Revenue vs profit Customer satisfaction vs frequency of purchase Social media followers by social media content publishing frequency
	Waterfall charts	Contributions to total sales by region Contributions to profit value Contributions to revenue by product
	Predictive forecasts	Sales forecasts Profit forecasts Customer-retention forecasts
	Geographical locations	Sales by county Usage by country Customers by postcode

149

Think about your users when selecting graphs: How data savvy are they? Are they data novices, and therefore do you need to keep the graphs to the simpler ones? Or are they data and statistical experts who would want to see the use of advanced graph types, so they can explore the data more fully?

Design the data visualisation for your specific users.

Building interactivity

Many users will want to interrogate data, so it often makes sense to incorporate interactivity and filtering into your data visualisations. Focus on the business requirements and what the user needs to do, in order to use the data to make smarter, quicker business decisions. Avoid adding a filter for every data field, as it could confuse your user(s).

Think about enabling users to slice and dice the data in different ways; for instance, doing one of the following:

- ✓ Filtering by date and/or time
- ✓ Filtering by department
- ✓ Filtering by customer
- ✓ Filtering by location
- ✓ Filtering by product
- ✓ Filtering by price and/or revenue

Consider enabling the users to see high-level statistics and then be able to dive into the detail; for instance, doing one of the following:

- ✓ Showing business-wide figures first, then enabling the users to view data by department and location if they want to
- ✓ Showing annual figures first, then enabling the users to view data by month and day if they want to
- ✓ Showing country-level figures first, then enabling the users to view by region, town and street if they want to

The exact form of interactivity will depend on this:

* *The purpose of your data visualisation and what's required for the user(s)*

* *The type of data you have access to and how much detail is available*

Filters can look confusing on a data visualisation, so I recommend putting all of your filters in one place to make them easy to see. For example, all filters could be shown on the right or left side of your data visualisation, or at the top. This makes it intuitive for a user, and it reduces the risk that they'll miss them.

Data visualisation tools

There are many data visualisation tools available on the market, and they each have pros and cons. The most frequently used tools are as follows:

Level	Description	Tools
Beginner	If your data is small and your visualisation needs are for individual graphs	Excel • Low cost • Widely used • Great introductory data tool
Intermediate	If your data is larger, and your visualisation needs are for scorecards, dashboards, reports, interactive tools, data extracts or insight stories	Power BI • Provided by Microsoft, it's a great, easy entry-level tool for Excel users Google Data Studio • This is a terrific tool if your data is predominately from Google Analytics or similar tools Tableau • This is designed for use by data-visualisation gurus • It's a more advanced tool with an array of specialist features

Level	Description	Tools
Advanced	If your data is big data, and your analytics needs are for AI, advanced predictions and discovery	R and Python • Both are programming languages • They require coding expertise

There are many more tools in addition to these. My team are regularly tracking 19 different data visualisation tools in terms of developing functionality, user experience and price, including these:

✓ Power BI Pro

✓ Domo

✓ Zoho

✓ Qlik

✓ Looker

✓ Mode

✓ Yellowfin

✓ ThoughtSpot

✓ Sisense

✓ MicroStrategy

✓ Spotfire

✓ Databox

✓ Klipfolio

✓ Cyfe

✓ PanIntelligence

✓ Metabase

These tools are developing, changing and improving all the time. Hence, it's important to keep an eye on the market and to select the right tool for your business requirements.

First impressions count

Whilst content is king – and a beautiful dashboard does not outweigh the need for accurate, valuable, intuitive data insight – first impressions do count. This means you should take the time to make your data visualisations look awesome.

Brand

- Use the right logos and colours for your business, in line with your brand guidelines
- Don't overwhelm the user with a rainbow of colours; select one dominant colour and one or two highlighter colours aligned to your brand, so it's easy to see the insight and trends
- Colour combinations should allow for colour-blindness, so be careful with red–green combinations
- Consider how data visualisations will work in black-and-white printed versions

Imagery

- Use images to enhance your design
- Keep it simple; don't let imagery get in the way of the data insight

Filters

- Put all filters in the same place and make sure they can be used in the same way
- Don't make them hard to find

Font

- Use a consistent font type and size
- Don't overwhelm the user with a crazy font selection

Text

- Remove any jargon or acronyms/initialisms
- Keep your text to a minimum so it's easy to read
- Use a text size that ensures the text is clearly legible in all areas; eg keys and axis titles
- Always spellcheck and grammar check all words (and by a real person as well as using the tools – the tools won't pick up typos such as 'from' instead of 'form'); you must NEVER have typos!

Labels

- Check all terminology is right for your users
- Apply the language your users use, not your own interpretation

Graphs

- The axes should clearly state the metric used; eg £, 000s or %
- Don't use the same type of graph for everything
- The title should explain clearly what's in the graph

White space

- Space out your visualisations so they're easy to see
- Don't overcrowd your data visualisations, as they will be hard to read

Alignment

- Whether it's centralised or left-orientated, make sure the alignment is the same throughout the visualisation

In all cases, keep it simple when it comes to delivery, and make it easy for the user to see what the data is telling them. A good design enhances a user experience. A bad design hinders a user experience. Make sure your design helps your user to understand the data insight.

Getting inspired

There are awesome data visualisations in the business world right now, so if you want some inspiration or new ideas, check out my favourites:

Information is beautiful:	https://informationisbeautiful.net/
The big book of dashboards:	www.bigbookofdashboards.com/
Microsoft Power BI Galleries:	https://community.powerbi.com/t5/Data-Stories-Gallery/bd-p/DataStoriesGallery
Tableau Public Gallery:	https://public.tableau.com/en-us/gallery/?tab=viz-of-the-dayandtype=viz-of-the-day

If in doubt, get started, have a play and ask for feedback; the more data visualisations you plan, design, build and use, the more you'll learn what works and what doesn't.

Testing is key at every stage, but particularly when you have created version one. Test the visualisations with users, iterate, retest, iterate, let the users get hands-on themselves, gather feedback and iterate again. If your data visualisation works, you'll get lots of feedback, and it will evolve continuously over time as it gets used more and more. If you hear nothing, it's probably failed.

Generating insight

Right at the start of this book, we talked about data being meaningless and actionable insight being the real source of business value. Therefore, it's crucial at this stage to challenge yourself: Do your data visualisations show actionable insight? Or are they just pretty pictures?

A way to test this is to ask yourself what you would recommend that the business should do differently based on the data visualisations you're sharing with them. Remember the three business levers from Step #2:

* *What should they start?*

* *What should they stop?*

* *What should they change?*

If you can't answer these questions, then you need to revisit your business requirements and check that your data visualisations are satisfying them. Have you missed a step? Have you lost focus along the way? Do you need to do some more work?

You can now visualise your data and share patterns, trends and insight with your business. You can feel confident using graphs, colour, icons and branding to personalise your data visualisation. You can show how insight is derived from the data and tell a data story to your user(s). Can you see how allowing sufficient time for data visualisations will result in a better user interface for your business?

Now the data tells you something, *it's insightful and actionable.*

REAL-WORLD EXAMPLE #7
A MARKETING AGENCY

I particularly wanted to share a data visualisation case study with you, as it's really tricky to create simple, intuitive data insight using graphs. So, let's bring the concepts explained in this step to life using this actual business-world example in the form of a marketing agency's experience with data visualisation.

THE BUSINESS

A marketing agency

THE DATA PROBLEM

This SME is an award-winning, independent marketing agency. With a UK headquarters, this agency has multiple departments, multiple client offerings, and multiple products and services. Like for many agencies, customer service is key, so key account client management activities are the core focus. The team members are mainly data novices, as are their customers, so making data simple is key. Its data covers campaigns, communications, coverage and response rates, all of which are stored in different places. The challenges here were disconnected data sources and manual data entry.

THE DATA OPPORTUNITY

- To automate the campaign reporting for clients, to reduce manual work

- To transform client reporting into beautiful visualisations

- To reduce risk in the business

THE DATA PROCESS

1. Business requirements – A workshop was run with the client-facing team to understand their business requirements for data visualisation.

2. Data review – The data sources and business processes were reviewed to understand what activities could be automated.

3. Mock-up – A visual design was created to check with the users that the business requirements were met and the branded design was acceptable before the live data visualisation was created.

4. Data visualisation – Specific graph types were selected to best represent the data available and make it easy for clients to interpret the data.

5. Data tool – Interactive, intuitive data visualisations were built in Power BI, which enabled the clients to slice and dice the data in a myriad of different ways, to satisfy their specific business requirements.

THE RESULT

A fully automated, client-facing data visualisation reporting tool was delivered. This saved the business time, significantly reduced the need for manual intervention and improved the quality of the client-facing data outputs.

THE STEP #7 DATA VISUALISATION TIP

For this business, the key element was providing data visualisation flexibility. Not all clients and businesses are the same, so there are good reasons why some data visualisations work for some clients and not for others. Providing the team with flexibility over the data visualisations, branding and graph types made sure that the client-reporting solution was future-proofed and scalable.

LESSONS LEARNT #7
VISUALISE YOUR DATA

During my career, I've acquired plenty of experience through aiding many businesses to visualise their data and create simple, intuitive and insightful data tools. This section details some of the errors businesses commonly make on Step #7 of the Data Escalator and what lessons can be learnt from them, so that you don't have to learn the hard way in your business.

1. THE USER IS THE ONLY PERSON WHO MATTERS

Rarely, if ever, can you create a data visualisation that everyone loves, so don't even try to. Focus on your specific user or users, and create a data visualisation that answers their questions and enables them to pull the right business levers once they have seen the insight. Throughout the design and development process for the data visualisation, make sure you have a single-minded focus on the specific user (or user role) you're building it for. Think about their thought process, what story you need to tell them and what questions they'll have. The user should be at the front of your mind throughout this step on the Data Escalator.

2. SHOWCASE THE INSIGHT, NOT THE DATA

On this step of the Data Escalator, it's all about delivering the data visualisation to support your data project's purpose specifically, and to help people decide what business levers they need to pull or push. Hence, show them insight, not data. Give them the sizzle, not the sausage. The data can be in the background in case they want to interrogate it. But the most important part of your data visualisation is to reveal clearly the actionable insight derived from your data project. Don't make it hard for them to find the insight – showcase it!

3. USE MOCK-UPS TO TEST YOUR DESIGN

I often draw data visualisations on paper or in PowerPoint first, before I even touch the data visualisation tool, just to double-check with the user that we're delivering the right solution for them. Often, it isn't until they see something that they realise what they described isn't necessarily what they actually wanted or that it doesn't quite work for them. This can save you a lot of time as it's far quicker to make changes at this stage, rather than at the end of the process. This investment in upfront planning time can improve the overall speed of your project.

4. SELECT THE RIGHT TOOL FOR THE JOB

There are many data visualisation tools out there, and they all have pros and cons. What's right for other businesses or other projects might not be right for your data project. When selecting the right data-visualisation tool for your specific data project, think about what you need to do and who you need to share it with.

5. A BEAUTIFUL DESIGN ALONE ≠ SUCCESS

Don't focus on design over substance. A pretty dashboard isn't enough. The design of your data visualisation should enhance your data insight, not hinder or confuse it. We've seen overly complex designs get in the way of powerful, valuable, simple data insight. Design with care.

You'll also learn your own lessons as your data visualisation work evolves, and you'll improve continually and grow in confidence as you do.

TASK #7 – CREATE YOUR DATA VISUALISATION PLAN

Before you continue, create a data visualisation plan for your next data project.

Take 10–20 minutes to start this now.

VISUALISATION PLANNING	YOUR ANSWERS
What key information do you want the user to take away after seeing the data insight?	
What data story do you want to tell them?	PART 1 –
	PART 2 –
	PART 3 –
	PART 4 –
What type of visualisation is required?	
What graphs are appropriate?	PART 1 –
	PART 2 –
	PART 3 –
	PART 4 –

VISUALISATION PLANNING	YOUR ANSWERS
What format will the data insight be in?	
What tool will be used?	

You can develop this further in the coming days, weeks and months of your data project.

Do you need a template or some help with this? Check out the Data Escalator Resources chapter at the end of the book.

STEP #8

MONETISE YOUR DATA

If there's no business benefit, why bother?

STEP #8 – MONETISE YOUR DATA

You've successfully planned, sourced, extracted, combined, processed, analysed and visualised your data, so what's next? Now's the time to consider if, how, when and where you can make or save more money for your business using data. Now's when your data strategy truly begins to impact your business strategy.

You need to challenge yourself at this stage. How can your data help your business to make or save more money? How can your data help you to make smarter, quicker business decisions? How can your data help your business to achieve your goals and KPIs? Is your data a business asset?

Use data to save money

Most businesses want to save money, and data can help you do this. There are two ways data can help a business to save money:

1. Data-specific cost savings

You could save money on your data architecture. Most businesses don't know how much money they're spending on their data architecture, and data-related technology, platforms and tools. This is because these costs are often split across different budgets and owned by different people, and therefore are hard to see all in one place. But there is a high likelihood that your business could be spending more on data than you're deriving value from the data. If so, there's a cost saving to be had.

The areas to consider are as follows:

a. *Are you storing every single type of data you collect?*

b. Are you storing data unnecessarily and incurring avoidable costs?

c. Are you duplicating costs through the same data being stored in different places?

d. Are you using expensive tools needlessly?

e. Are you paying for data tools that you're not using?

The best way to answer these questions is to run a data audit to identify all data-associated costs across your business, so you can do the following:

✓ Prioritise the highest costs

✓ Identify alternative options

✓ Decide what to stop, start and/or change

Can you save money from making data-specific cost savings? Find out using this data-specific cost-saving template:

DATA SOURCE	DATA TYPE	BUSINESS PURPOSE	BUSINESS USAGE	BUSINESS VALUE	MONTHLY COST
SAGE/Xero	Financial	Log incoming and outgoing cash	HIGH	HIGH	£X
HubSpot	Customer	Log contacts and orders	LOW	HIGH	£X
AWS/GCP	Operation	Data warehouse	LOW	HIGH	£X

Do you need a template or some help with this? Check out the Data Escalator Resources chapter at the end of the book.

2. Business cost savings

You could save money in other areas within your business, beyond data-related costs. You can use data to identify where a business can save money. You can use data analysis to get a clear view of all your spend across your business. You may identify areas where money is being wasted, tasks that are being duplicated, work that's inefficient or where the rate of return is too low for the investment.

Areas to consider are as follows:

* *Do you have a clear view of spend by time, region, product, team, department, etc.?*

* *Are you duplicating spend across your business?*

* *Are you generating enough ROI for your spend?*

The best way to answer these questions is to run a data audit to identify all costs across your business, so you can do the following:

✓ Prioritise the highest costs

✓ Assess the commercial value that a specific spend brings to the business (eg increased sales)

✓ Identify alternative options

✓ Decide what to stop, start and/or change

Can you save money from business cost savings? Find out using this business-cost-saving template, which is on the next page.

Do you need a template or some help with this? Check out the Data Escalator Resources chapter at the end of the book.

COST TYPE	COST DESCRIPTION	MONTHLY COST	IMPACT ON SALES	EXPECTED MONTHLY SALES REDUCTION
PEOPLE	Employees	£100,000	Sales teams stop	£200,000
	Contractors	£15,000	None	–
PROPERTY	Rent	£2,000	None	–
TECHNOLOGY		£1,000	Minor	–
TRAVEL		£3,000	Client visits	£10,000
EXPENSES		£500	None	–

In our experience, businesses can reduce costs by at least 10% of their budgets using data. When this is combined over years of expenditure, it can make a big difference to your bottom line. And a quick win like this can be a major coup to win the hearts and minds of your leadership team.

Use data to make money

Most or all businesses want to make more money, and data can help you do this. Data insight can enable businesses to win new clients, retain high-value clients, grow clients and expand into new markets.

For instance, it will help you to do the following:

- See where there's high and low performance, so you can target resources and budget in the right places

- Use AI to identify patterns and trends you can't easily see, so you can discover something new about your business

- Understand who your highest-value customers are, so you can retain high-value customers, convert mid- or low-value customers to high-value customers or terminate them, and offer special offers / loyalty schemes to increase customer value

- Target sales and marketing activity to current or potential high-value customers, so you can ensure that your sales and marketing budgets deliver a higher ROI

- Track your sales funnel and conversion rates at each stage, so you can implement specific activities to improve problem areas

- Track your customer journey (usage; engagement; satisfaction; retention rates; and customer pause, loss and exit rates), so you can implement specific activities to improve problem areas

Another way to look at how data can help your business to make more money is to use data to analyse your performance along your customer journey. Firstly, you need to map out your customer journey. You can take weeks and months to do this to a super-high level of detail, if you want to, or you can create a simplified version, as we have done in an hour:

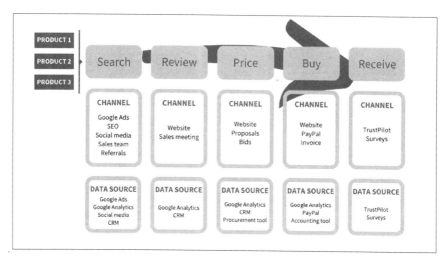

Figure 7: Customer journey data analytics example

This simplified customer journey enables you to see your customer's steps, the channels you use to communicate with customers, and the data sources you use, all on one page. This is a great way to focus your mind on what's important for data analysis.

Then you need to collect data on each of the stages in your customer journey, from all the data sources you can:

STAGE	CHANNEL	METRIC	JAN 2020	FEB 2020	MAR 2020	APR 2020
SEARCH	Google Ads	Clicks	50	60	70	80
		Impressions	4,000	5,000	6,000	8,000
	Google Analytics	Home-page views	125	156	178	120
		Session duration	0:12	0:19	0:24	0:10
	Twitter	Likes/ followers	300	310	320	330
REVIEW	Google Analytics	Product-page views (for each product)	125	156	178	120
		Session durations (for each product)	0:12	0:19	0:24	0:10
PRICE		Price-page views (for each product)	125	156	178	120
		Session durations (for each product)	0:12	0:19	0:24	0:10
		Conversions (for each product)	2%	1.5%	1%	2%
BUY	PayPal	Basket	10	12	9	8
		Purchase completed	5	5	4	8
RECEIVE	Survey	Customer satisfaction	90%	95%	99%	98%

Figure 8: Customer journey data analytics example

I recommend limiting this analysis to a defined time period – for instance, the last three months – so you don't get tied down with lots of data. However, if your business is seasonal, or if you've experienced a particularly good or bad patch, you may need to look at data for a longer time period.

Then you can use the data to identify where your customer journey is working well and where it isn't:

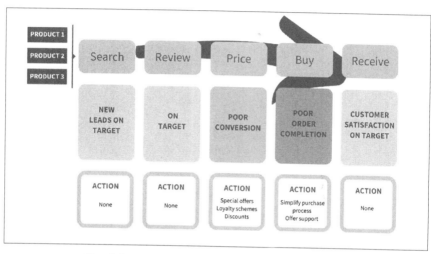

Figure 9: Customer journey showing potential data-driven actions

This will enable you to see where your problem areas are, as well as revealing the high-performing areas. You can then focus your time, effort and money in the places that will generate the most returns for your business, and stop wasting time or budget in other areas.

These data-driven actions will enable you to monetise data indirectly, through making quicker, smarter, data-informed decisions, so you'll win, retain and grow your clients and your profit. But what about monetising your data directly?

Packaging data into a new product

Data is the new oil! Data monetisation! Everyone talks about it, but few businesses do it. However, particularly in the current climate, wouldn't a brand-new source of revenue be helpful to your business? Now we're not saying every business can monetise its data directly, as the more data you have, the greater the opportunity, of course. It's still well worth any business considering its ability to monetise its data.

Firstly, you need to think of your data as an asset; data can seem amorphous, vague and opaque. If you don't like spreadsheets, numbers or coding, it could terrify you. So, the best way to start is to break down your data into its component parts: think customer profiles, social media, feedback surveys, telephone calls, online behaviour and more.

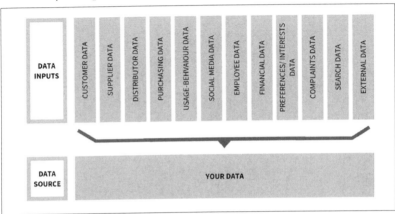

Secondly, you need to get creative with how your data could be repackaged into a completely new format, for a completely new audience, with a completely new objective. Monetising data doesn't mean selling email addresses to dubious third parties; it could mean creating new indices, dashboards, predictive tools, market-trend reports and so on.

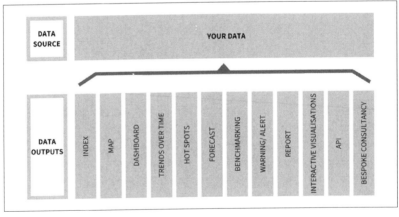

Figures 10 & 11: Examples of data inputs and data outputs

Using data you already have, you could create brand-new data products and services, and hence new revenue streams for your business. This could be for either current customers or new ones. It could be in the form of a dashboard, benchmark or forecast, for instance.

Do you need a template or some help with this? Check out the Data Escalator Resources chapter at the end of the book.

Build new data products for your customers

Many businesses are, or could be, building brand-new data products and services for their existing clients, distributors, suppliers and/or intermediaries – and they charge an additional fee for it. This could create a new source of revenue for a business, using data it already has.

Here are some examples:

- Dashboard

  Show your customers their product or service usage over time

  - For instance, retailers provide a dashboard demonstrating past orders and loyalty points

- Comparisons

  Reveal to your customers how they compare to other people like them

  - For instance, energy suppliers illustrate how your energy usage compares to other households of a similar size, location and number of residents

- Benchmarking

  Rank your customers against other customers on an anonymised basis o   For instance, computer games or karting tracks often do this by showing your score on a scoreboard

- Predictions

  Provide a forecast for customers on their future usage of your product(s) or service(s)

        o   For instance, Google predicts how busy a shop will be based on past activity or footfall

- What-if-scenario planning

  Show customers what would happen if they made a change to their product or service

        o   For instance, mortgage providers demonstrate your final repayment amount and how it changes depending on your monthly repayments

There are two ways to deliver these new data products to your customers:

1. **Integrate your new data product into your existing customer platform or user interface**

2. **Build a new, separate user interface for your new data product**

The right decision for your business will depend on whether you have an existing customer platform, and if you do, how happy you are with it. A separate user interface is often quicker to build, as you don't have to worry about integration with the existing platform, but it can result in a confusing user journey for your customers. This means it's important to make the right decision for your business. I always recommend building a prototype first for test purposes and separate from your existing customer platform, so you can seek customer feedback, test it properly and finalise the design before integrating it with your existing customer platform.

Build new data products for new markets

To diversify their business and increase their revenue using data they already have, many businesses could sell data insight products and services to new customer segments, to new markets and to new customers.

Here are some examples:

- Trend reports

  Provide new insight to your market using anonymised, aggregated data

  - o For instance, CB Insights provides reports on the technology sectors
  - o For instance, research organisations and think tanks provide reports on specialised topics

- Market indices

  Create a new metric for your market in the format of an index, quadrant, score or KPI

  - o For instance, Gartner shares quadrants to compare technology solutions
  - o For instance, there are indices for house prices and rental prices

- Advertising space

  Other businesses can promote products and services to your customers through your website, emails and events

  - o For instance, sponsored website banners or sponsored emails

- Data sales

  Provide access to your data to third parties through an application programming interface (API) or lists

  o For instance, businesses such as Crunchbase and Equifax sell data on businesses

There could be many ways for you to productise data within your business. It's important to think creatively and innovatively at this stage. Look beyond your market sector and region for inspiration. Think of your individual data fields and data sources as assets. Don't just do what you've always done; think differently. Don't just copy what others are doing; look for ways to lead your market. This process can be hard for a business to accomplish internally. At this stage, it may be right to bring in external help to inspire new thinking and to push for innovation.

The right product opportunity for your business will depend on four things:

1. *What data do you have available? How rich is it? Is it unique? Is it at a large enough scale to be valuable?*

2. *What permissions do you have for the data? Have you got permission to use the data in the ways you want to?*

3. *What market(s) are you targeting? What will people use, value and buy?*

4. *What else is available in your target market(s)? What do people use today? Is there a gap?*

Your business could create a brand-new unique selling point (USP) and competitive advantage for your business using data.

Do you need a template or some help with this? Check out the Data Escalator Resources chapter at the end of the book.

Consider strategic data partnerships

If you don't have much data yourself – perhaps if you're a small business or start-up – you should consider strategic data partnerships. Find other businesses who sell to the same people or businesses that you do, but who aren't your direct competitors. Think about an events organiser, photographer, hotel manager and florist – all are selling to couples planning their weddings. Think about a marketing agency, accountant, lawyer and website designer – all are selling to SMEs. By working together, you could all win by sharing:

* Customer data (if you have permission to share your data with third parties)

* Advertising space (eg website banners, sponsored emails and blogs) to reach customers

Whatever business you're in and whatever data you have, spend some time pondering how you can monetise it. You could be surprised at what you come up with.

How much money could you make?

There is no easy answer to this. One byte of data does not always equal £10, for instance. Therefore, the best way to answer this is using six questions:

#	QUESTION	EXAMPLE
1.	What are you going to sell? Is it a report, a dashboard, a new index, a graph, survey results, etc.?	Dashboard
2.	Who will buy it? An individual or a business? Who are they? Where are they?	Current business customers
3.	How many customers could you target in year one?	100
4.	What will they pay for it?	£10,000 per year

#	QUESTION	EXAMPLE
5.	How many could you sell in year one?	20
6	So how much could you earn in year one?	£200,000

Clearly, you'll need to make assumptions and guesstimates in this process, but I'm sure you can see that this needs to be customer-focused – your data insight is only worth what people will pay for it.

You've now successfully planned, sourced, extracted, combined, processed, analysed, visualised and monetised your data. Your data strategy is impacting your business strategy directly. You're helping your business to make or save more money. You're facilitating your business making smarter, quicker business decisions. You're assisting your business to achieve your goals and KPIs. Can you see how data is a valuable business asset?

Now there's a business benefit, *it's worth the effort.*

REAL-WORLD EXAMPLE #8
AN EMPLOYEE BENEFITS BUSINESS

Monetising data sounds easy, but it's hard to do in practice because you have to ensure that your data monetisation is legally compliant and customer friendly, as well as being a commercial opportunity. Consequently, I wanted to provide a data monetisation case study that converts the principles described in this step into a practical, tactical example to give a real-world view.

THE BUSINESS

An employee benefits business

THE DATA PROBLEM

This business is a high-growth, private SME. The business has a traditional structure and is split into functional departments. It has a core client offering, but with a range of optional product features, add-on modules and supporting services. Due to working with large business employers in the public and private sectors, key account client management activity is critical. This business is technology led, with hundreds of business clients and years of data. Its data covers employers, employees and employee benefit usage, and it's largely stored in one place. Maximising the value from its existing data is the main challenge for this business.

THE DATA OPPORTUNITY

- To create a new competitive advantage in a crowded, competitive market

- To win, retain and grow clients using data already available within the business

- To generate a new source of revenue

THE DATA PROCESS

1. Business requirements – A workshop was run with a multi-functional team to understand the business requirements for client-facing data analytics.

2. Data review – The data sources and business processes were reviewed to understand what data was available and how it could be analysed.

3. Prototype – Working with a data extract and not live data, a series of prototypes were created that showed the potential data analytics and data visualisations that could be valuable to clients.

4. Testing – The prototypes were tested with the internal team and with the target clients. Feedback was used to improve and develop the prototypes.

5. Automation – Automated data analytics and data visualisations were created for the clients. These were interactive, intuitive tools that enabled the clients to slice and dice the data in a multitude of different ways, to satisfy their specific business requirements.

THE RESULT

A new data analytics and data visualisation product for clients that can be sold for additional fees. This was a new, differentiated, competitive offering for the employee benefits market, for both current clients and new clients.

THE STEP #8 DATA MONETISATION TIP

For this business, the key element was building prototypes using sample data. This allowed ideas to be tested rapidly, iterated, refined and tested again. This prototype-led approach allowed new ideas to be tested with minimal effort and before spending a lot of time building the final data product. This saved time and costs, and it facilitated the innovative data product being launched to market quickly. It also provided the opportunity for the target clients to inform the design of the data product before it was finalised, which was a terrific way to engage the early customers.

LESSONS LEARNT #8
MONETISE YOUR DATA

The information presented in this book is based on my own practical experience, including that gained through helping many businesses to monetise their data and to generate brand-new revenue streams. Hopefully, by me detailing some of the slip-ups I have encountered and the resulting lessons learnt, you will be able to avoid making the same mistakes in your business on Step #8 of the Data Escalator.

1. THINK COMMERCIAL

Up until now, your stakeholders might have been technical or operational people. But now you need to think commercially and engage potentially different stakeholders: sales, product and strategy teams, and the board. At this point, it's all about the money; talk to the people who want to make or save money. Make it simple for them, as they might not understand data. Speak their language. Show them examples and mock-ups, and give them some financial forecasts to make the money-making potential real to them.

2. GET CREATIVE

When it comes to monetising data, most people think of selling lists with customer details to unscrupulous third parties and, obviously, they don't want to do that. But there are so many other ways to package data up in different forms. Think of all your data sources as individual boxes of data and imagine building new products using different combinations of those data boxes. I run workshops just like this to enable businesses to get creative with data, and it works with data novices, data scientists and through to the board.

3. THINK BEYOND YOUR CURRENT MARKET

Your money-making data opportunities might exist beyond your current customer base. It could involve your current suppliers, distributers or intermediaries. Or there could be opportunities in a market that is brand new to you. Don't be constrained by what you've done in the past. Think of your data as an asset, and consider who would value the insight that could be generated from it and how they'd use it.

4. DO YOUR RESEARCH

Before you get too excited and spend lots of time, effort and money on creating a new data product, do your research. Review competitor offerings, speak to your target customers, test a prototype and seek feedback early. If you're thinking of entering a new market, consider using an expert in that market to inform your development plans. Make sure you know as much as you can before you invest in new product development.

5. KEEP IT LEGAL

Whatever you do with your data, make sure you've thought it through, put yourself in the minds of your customers, and ticked all the legal requirements. You don't want to inadvertently create a problem for your business later down the road. Run a data protection impact assessment. Check your terms and conditions to guarantee that you're working within the rules you've agreed with your customers. Obtain legal advice if you're unsure.

You'll also learn your own lessons as your data monetisation work evolves, and you'll improve continually and grow in confidence as you do.

TASK #8 – CREATE YOUR DATA MONETISATION PLAN

Now create some data monetisation ideas for your data project.

Take 10–20 minutes to start this now.

MONETISATION PLANNING	YOUR ANSWERS
IDEA #1	
What data do you have?	
How could you package it together into a new product?	
Who would buy it?	
Why would they buy it?	
How much would they pay for it?	
How much revenue could your business make?	
IDEA #2	
What data do you have?	
How could you package it together into a new product?	
Who would buy it?	
Why would they buy it?	
How much would they pay for it?	
How much revenue could your business make?	

MONETISATION PLANNING	YOUR ANSWERS
IDEA #3	
What data do you have?	
How could you package it together into a new product?	
Who would buy it?	
Why would they buy it?	
How much would they pay for it?	
How much revenue could your business make?	

You can develop this further in the coming days, weeks and months of your data project.

Do you need a template or some help with this? Check out the Data Escalator Resources chapter at the end of the book.

GO RIDE THE DATA ESCALATOR

Well done, you have successfully glided up the eight steps of the Data Escalator!

You can now design, plan, lead, manage, test and launch your own data project within your business, using the knowledge gained from the eight steps:

#	STEP	NOW YOU CAN...
1.	UNDERSTAND YOUR BUSINESS NEEDS	Plan your data project so it's purposeful, and so the insight generated is actionable and valuable
2.	DEFINE YOUR DATA STRATEGY	Create a data strategy that's aligned to your business strategy and sets out a clear vision for your business to achieve
3.	MAP YOUR DATA SOURCES	Identify, review and map your data sources so you understand what data you can play with
4.	CONNECT YOUR DATA	Manage the extraction, transformation and load of your data, then connect it all together
5.	PROCESS YOUR DATA	Check, sort and store your data so it's ready for analysis
6.	ANALYSE YOUR DATA	Slice and dice your data to discover new patterns and trends
7.	VISUALISE YOUR DATA	Visualise your data to present intuitive designs to your target users
8.	MONETISE YOUR DATA	Use your data to make or save more money, in a legally compliant and customer-focused way

You're ready, and now it's your turn…

✓ *You've created your data strategy…*

✓ *You've got a data plan…*

✓ *You know where to extract your data from…*

✓ *You know what your users require…*

✓ *You know what tools you are going to use…*

✓ *You have some ideas for data visualisation…*

✓ *You're ready to get started…*

So now you'll need some help.

I recommend working with a multi-skilled team on any data project, as no one person can do it all. For any data project, you need skills ranging from consultancy and client management, to coding and engineering experience, through to data visualisation and insight generation. Rarely, if ever, do you find one person who's experienced, capable and motivated in all of these areas. Hence, a team approach using individual skills and experience is the right approach for most data projects.

There are six key roles in any data project:

1. The data consultant

The data consultant's role is to translate between the technical team and the business. They need to have enough understanding of data engineering to make it simple for the business. They must make data simple. They need to act as a go-between with data engineers/architects and business users. They have to translate business requirements into technical requirements. And they must be prepared to answer questions from either side. These people are rare, as most people are either technical or business orientated.

The skills required for a data consultant are as follows:

- **Commercial** – They understand how a business makes money

- **New product development** – They understand how to turn data into business-facing solutions

- **Data governance** – They know that data processes need to be robust, secure and compliant

- **Leadership** – They're confident being the person accountable for a data project's success

2. The data architect

The data architect's role is to design the right solution, and ensure it's robust, secure and scalable. This person needs to use the business requirements to design the right data architecture for a given project. They must consider known and defined current requirements, as well as undefined and unknown future requirements. They have to apply their learnings from past projects to make certain that the data architecture is flexible, scalable and future-proofed.

The skills required for a data architect are as follows:

- **Engineering** – They have tons of experience designing, building, testing, launching and managing data architectures

- **Data warehouse design** – They understand what good data warehouse solutions look like, how they vary, and the pros and cons of data warehousing

- **Data-workflow design** – They know how to plan and build data pipelines, so data is stored and transferred robustly and successfully

3. The data wrangler

The data wrangler's role is to ETL data. This could involve multiple data sources, in different formats and from different locations. This person needs to be hands-on and happy working down in the detail of getting data into one place. They need to be a problem-solver and a trouble-shooter, and relish finding solutions to a variety of challenges that come up along the way.

The skills required for a data wrangler are as follows:

- **ETL** – They're confident extracting, transforming and loading data

- **Python/SQL** – They can use code to change the format of data and apply business logic

- **APIs** – they know how to connect to data from different third-party platforms

4. The data analyst

The data analyst's role is to analyse the data, and to find new patterns and trends. This person needs to be naturally curious, always asking questions and keen to find out more. They need to be customer-orientated, and be focused on how data analysis can help solve a business problem or support a new business opportunity.

The skills required for a data analyst are as follows:

- **Requirements gathering** – They work with the stakeholders to determine what the scope and business requirements are, and then dive into the details of the business requirements to ensure they fully understand the business value of potential data insight

- **Analytics** – They're able to slice and dice data in different ways to show various trends

- **Statistics** – They know how to use models to test, validate and prove the patterns found in the data

5. The data scientist

The data scientist's role is to create advanced AI and predictive models. This person needs to build on the knowledge gained through standard data analytics and go deeper into the data. This person must be an expert in statistics and data modelling, and know how to apply these tools to specific business problems, so the insight gained is meaningful and actionable.

The skills required for a data scientist are as follows:

- **Statistics** – They know how and when to create statistical data models

- **AI** – They're able to apply AI methodologies to data problems

- **ML** – They have experience of applying ML approaches to create predictive models

- **NLP** – They're used to applying NLP to unstructured data

- **Coding** – They're experienced in using coding languages, such as R, in a data-science capacity

6. The data visualiser

The data visualiser's role is to create intuitive user interfaces. This person needs to be someone who's both highly visual and user orientated. They need to be able to make complex data simple. They're focused on how a user can benefit from seeing the data, and will give them exactly the tools they need. The result is a simple, intuitive and sometimes beautiful dashboard, report or graph.

The skills required for a data visualiser are as follows:

- **Data storytelling** – they're great at making data simple for their users

- **Design** – they love making data look easy-to-understand and stylish

- **User-interface development** – they plan, build and test data tools for their users

- **Insight** – they're experienced at deriving the 'so what' and user value from data

- **Data visualisation tools** – They're confident using data visualisation tools, such as Power BI, Tableau and Qlik

What type of data person are you?

Most people usually put themselves into one of these six types of data role or sometimes two. But, in our experience, rarely would someone put themselves into all six roles. Think about what you're good at, what your experience has included and what you love to do. Put yourself in that role, and then find the rest of your data team to help you.

No single person can do everything when it comes to data

I recommend that you bring together a team of data experts who can each play their own specific role in your data project. Every project we work on has multiple data experts involved, at different stages and for different time periods, as no single data expert is the best person for every aspect of a data project. It's a team effort. And if you need any help, ask me.

Email hello@thedataescalator.com

By riding the eight steps of the Data Escalator, you're now able to do the following:

✓ *Create a data strategy and data plan for your business*
✓ *Launch your first data project*
✓ *Know what good looks like*

Good luck with your data project, and let me know how you get on:

✓ *Share your Data Escalator stories with me*
✓ *Give me feedback*
✓ *Ask questions*

RESOURCES

* *Do you need some help?*

* *Do you want to see some real-life examples?*

* *Do you need access to practical hands-on data tools and templates?*

* *Are you looking for inspiration?*

Check out our online resources at www.thedataescalator.com

Here, you'll find the following:

✓ The FREE templates mentioned in this book

✓ FREE online tools

✓ Sector-specific templates

✓ Department-specific templates

✓ Case studies

✓ Tool comparisons

✓ Frequently asked questions

✓ News and alerts

✓ Webinars

✓ Online training videos

Get access for free via the website or email hello@thedataescalator.com

---

ABOUT THE AUTHOR

Helen is a data fanatic. With a career born in the corporate world, she honed her commercial and technical skills in government organisations and global corporate giants before setting up Data³, the data lab, in 2017.

An oceanography and geography graduate from the University of Southampton and University College London, respectively, Helen's first role was at the Met Office. This involved spending days, if not weeks, at sea, changing meteorological sensors on offshore weather buoys and then analysing the data back on land. Not for the seasick! After some time travelling in Asia and working at the Australian Bureau of Meteorology in Melbourne, Helen moved to the commercial part of the Met Office. It was here that Helen really got into the money-making aspect of data; in this case, selling weather forecasts to the largest retailers and insurers in the UK. Is it going to be a sunny bank holiday weekend in two weeks' time, so the supermarkets need to stock up on BBQ goods? Did a storm really cause all that damage to that one business property last month? These were the questions that weather data answered in the form of predictive and historical data products.

From there, Helen moved into the commercial world of financial services, which was quite a jump. Whilst working at AXA and Computershare, Helen succeeded in a range of marketing, sales and product-orientated roles, always being passionate about the use of business data to drive growth and make businesses money.

And then came the lightbulb moment: why help all these big, global corporations with data when she could help SMEs? Inspired by her dad's experience running engineering businesses in Swindon, Wiltshire, Helen has grown increasingly passionate about supporting SMEs with respect to their data needs and helping them to play with the big-business tools on a tight budget. Consequently, in March 2017, she set up Data[3].

ABOUT DATA³

Whatever type of business you're in, you'll have a lot of data. Customer details, financials, sales figures – the list goes on. This data is pivotal when it comes to making decisions on ways you can improve what you do, save time and make more money. However, what you might not have is data you can trust – or the skills to make the most of it. That's where Data³ comes in.

Data³ is the UK data lab. They make data simple. They know how to make data manageable, they understand how to make it accessible to everyone, and they recognise how to use it to save you time and money.

Data³ works with businesses that want more insight into their organisation or customers, but that don't have the right data skills, enough time in the day or enough money to hire full-time staff. Think of Data³ like a data SWAT team – a band of consultants, engineers, analysts and visualisers who turn your data into stories and help your business to grow.

With a headquarters in Bristol, UK, Data³ has a growing team that has extended from Bristol, to Swindon, to London, to the Isle of Man and to the United Arab Emirates, and with global growth plans.

THE DATA³ TEAM

It takes a village to raise a book – and this one is no exception. This was a real team effort, and the key contributors include the following:

* **Tristan Dibbens** – our data architecture guru

* **Amanda Kite** – our insight-generating visualisation expert

* **Matt Dent** – our business intelligence ninja

* **Helen Ward** – our strategic marketing consultant

Find out more about Data³ and the team at https://data-cubed.co.uk/